DESIGN FOR BELONGING

DESIGN FOR BELONGING

How to Build Inclusion and Collaboration in Your Communities

Susie Wise
Illustrations by Rose Jaffe

TEN SPEED PRESS
California | New York

HASSO PLATTNER
Institute of Design at Stanford

For Mariah and Victor, thank you for pointing the way. You inspire me beyond these words. And to Frazer and Hattie, for everything.

Contents

A Note from the d.school

At the Stanford d.school, *design* is a verb. It's an attitude to embody and a way to work. The core of that work is trying, to the best of one's abilities, to help things run more smoothly, delight more people, and ease more suffering. This holds true for you, too—whether design is your profession or simply a mindset you bring to life.

Founded in 2005 as a home for wayward thinkers, the d.school was a place where independent-minded people could gather, try out ideas, and make change. A lot has shifted in the decade or so since, but that original exuberant and resourceful attitude is as present today as it was then.

Our series of guides is here to offer you the same inventiveness, insight, optimism, and perseverance that we champion at the d.school. Like a good tour guide, these handbooks will help you find your way through unknown territory and introduce you to some fundamental ideas that we hope will become cornerstones in your creative foundation.

Circumvent your fears and do the work that matters to you in *Drawing on Courage*. Delve into the unknown to find new opportunity in *Navigating Ambiguity*. And in this book, learn to build inclusive communities where everybody has room to collaborate and flourish.

Welcome to *Design for Belonging*!

love,
the d.school

Welc

Open to explore moments to notice and investigate.

thrive in their new communities. Having a sense of belonging leads to flourishing in every environment and group, big and small, from your home to the culture at large.

Belonging helps us to be fully human. It gives us permission to share our talents and express our life force. It enables cooperation, collaboration, and the ability to work across difference. It emboldens our creativity and our problem-solving abilities. When people feel like they belong, they are able to be their best and do their best.

Design has the power to change things for the better, to address historic wrongs created through exclusionary design processes. If you want to create change, you've gotta make something. But you don't have to call yourself a designer to benefit from the information in this book; you just have to use its tools to make things happen. Whether you are a parent, manager, teacher, community organizer, or leader of almost any sort, you can design a space that helps people feel they belong. And that's what I explore in this book: the intersection of belonging and design. I like to express this intersection as "belonging + design" because it suggests that the process is additive, that we're building something bigger. In this sense, belonging + design = new ways of bringing people together, or even new ways of *being* people together.

So how do you design for belonging? In the coming pages, I'll explore three essential elements: the feeling of belonging, the moments during which belonging occurs, and the process of shaping your context so belonging can emerge.

Acknowledging that belonging is a feeling is a powerful way to start this work. While you can't design a feeling—feelings are personal—you *can* learn to recognize how and when feelings arise and then design all sorts of things that positively influence those feelings: rituals that bring us together, spaces that keep us calm, roles that create a sense of responsibility, systems that make us feel respected, communications that create understanding, and more. You can also identify the key moments during which we experience the world and intentionally shape them into experiences of belonging. You use these moments to help set the stage for belonging to emerge.

To provoke your thinking and support your exploration, I will introduce a crew of thinkers and doers who represent diverse frameworks for belonging. I've dubbed this group the "host-heroes of belonging" in the spirit of writer and organizational thinker Margaret Wheatley, who encouraged leaders to see themselves not as *heroes* to save others, but rather as *hosts* who bring people together to begin conversations and launch critical actions. For me, these brilliant people are both notable hosts for an emerging conversation about the possibilities of belonging and also my personal heroes because of how their work has influenced me—sometimes up close and personal and sometimes purely as a consumer of their work. From movies and media they have created to the scholarship and interventions they have deployed, their work stimulates new ideas for what and how to design. You saw them in the mural that opened this introduction, and you'll be hearing more from them throughout the book.

You'll also find stories of what it is like to grapple with the feelings of belonging and its often-powerful opposite, othering, as well as exercises you can use to explore belonging and othering in your world. The stories shared are those of real people. Some I have worked with extensively; some I only met in brief interactions or interviews. Many names are changed; some are not.

An additional note about language: Many current publishing style guides refer to *Black people* and *white people*. In this work, I use the phrases *Black people* and *White people* when using racial identifiers. I am following the call of Eve Ewing and others to capitalize White. As she has said, not capitalizing white along with Black "runs the risk of reinforcing the dangerous myth that White people in America do not have a racial identity." This is part of the ongoing effort to recognize that White people are situated within our racialized power structures and need to be held accountable for helping to dismantle White supremacy.

And while words clearly matter, design is not just words. It is active. And I want to help you actively build belonging in your life, your work, your community, and in our world. I invite you to use this book in ways that work for you. Write in it. Add pages to it. Make a mess of it. Or keep it crisp and clean, if that's your preference. There are lots of questions and exercises for you to dig into, try out, and pass along to others. My hope is that you will use *Design for Belonging* as a powerful tool to invite collaboration to create the change you need to see in your world.

Let's get started.

Feel

ing

Belonging

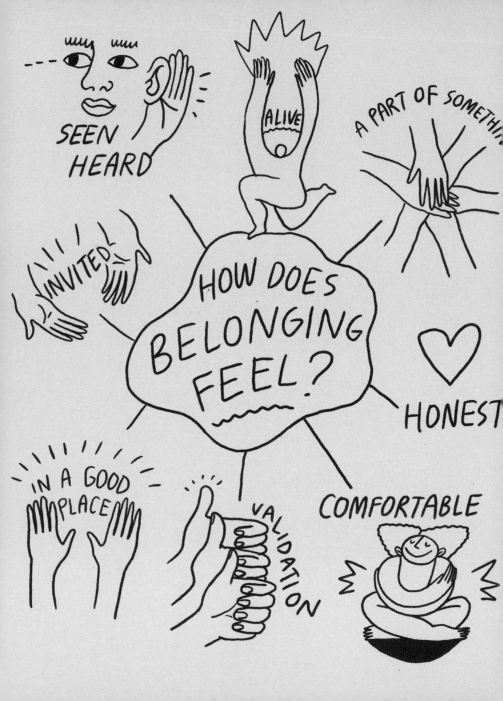

Belonging and Othering

There are many definitions of belonging and its insistent opposing force, othering. *Belonging* is being accepted and invited to participate; being part of something and having the opportunity to show up as yourself. More than that, it means being able to raise issues and confront harsh truths as a full member of a community. *Othering*, by contrast, is treating people from another group as essentially different from and generally inferior to the group you belong to. Once these terms enter your frame of reference, you'll find that belonging and othering show up everywhere: at the mall, in the pick-up line at your child's school, in the rhetoric of national politics. You can't *not* see them (double negative intended).

What belonging means for you is likely different from what it means for me. What belonging is for each of us also changes depending on the context. The same is true for othering—the way it feels can vary wildly. Take a look at the mind maps here. They give us starting points for exploring belonging and othering in all of their complexity and in your life, work, and communities.

Although the maps only scratch the surface of what belonging and othering can mean, they illustrate that a lot of powerful and important feelings are wrapped up in these concepts.

I was first introduced to belonging and othering in the work of john a. powell (page 64). A lawyer by training, powell leads the Othering & Belonging Institute at the University of California, Berkeley, where he and a team work with folks across health, education, housing, transportation policy, and the cultural arts to make good on the promise of civil rights. At the time, I was working with high school principals across the United States in some of our country's most segregated school environments, in a program called School Retool, which sought to introduce school leaders to design thinking tools and deeper learning practices to make their schools more learner centered. In this process I found myself wondering how we might support leaders in bringing their equity agendas front and center. As these leaders were becoming empowered by the tools and mindsets of design, could they also use their energy to address the needs of those students furthest from opportunity? Specifically, I thought about Steve, an assistant principal at a Denver middle school who was struggling to engage students and support them in building relationships across racial and economic lines. He knew the status quo wasn't serving the kids, he thought it could be different in his school, and yet he didn't have concrete ideas for how to help make change happen.

When I shared some of powell's work with educators like Steve, the othering and belonging framework unlocked an understanding of how to make progress on the equity challenges they were confronting. In simple terms, powell's ideas made belonging the goal to shoot for. The educators could use their creativity to imagine what would build more belonging for and among the students, and they could be laser focused on the experiences and structures that were othering individuals or groups. This meant a shift from

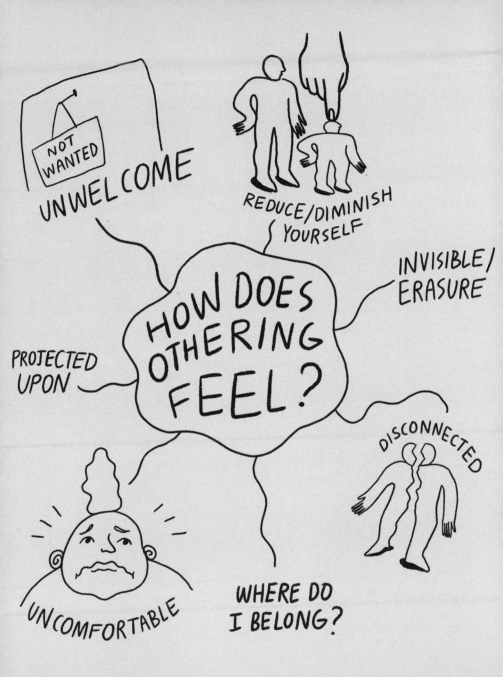

looking at diversity, equity, and inclusion (DEI) as a technical problem to be solved through data and numbers to seeing it as a relational opportunity to connect with the people in their communities. With this shift to using belonging and othering as a framework for seeing what was happening in their schools, leaders were able to get very clear about the work they needed to do. For example, with increased belonging as a goal, one principal focused with renewed energy on connecting with parents of students of color; another created ways to support new teachers in getting to know the students they were serving; yet another got brave enough to confront the data they had around discipline and its disproportionate impact on students of color.

The shift from fixing something as a technical endeavor to recognizing the human need to belong as relational work is also something I saw up close when working with Victor Cary at the National Equity Project, an educational consulting organization that teaches and coaches leading-for-equity programs across the country. Victor brilliantly coaches leaders (including me!—it was Victor who first handed me an article by powell) by cutting directly to the heart of a matter with feedback like, "That's great, but it sounds kind of technical. What was really going on? What were the people involved feeling? And was there anything predictable about who was feeling what?" Digging into feelings is about picking up signals of tension in any situation. Not shying away from feelings—and not ignoring signs of othering—gives you powerful fuel to promote greater belonging and reduce othering across a wide range of contexts.

How Belonging Feels

Belonging is the invitation to be your full self, however that looks. It is the opportunity—no matter who you are—to learn, live, and love, to be honored, encouraged, and allowed to develop as *you* and as part of the groups that develop and celebrate your identities, needs, and contributions.

People often speak casually about a "sense of belonging." Victor Cary insists that we call it a "sense" because we feel belonging and othering in our bodies. Your body knows the tingle of being truly seen and the shrinking devastation of being turned away. Indeed, our individual situations may vary greatly, but collectively we know personally what it feels like to belong and to be othered as well.

"You need a felt acquaintance of the equity challenge you are confronting. In many cases you need to put yourself into the system so you can see and feel what is happening."

—VICTOR CARY

VICTOR CARY

Victor Cary is a senior director with the National Equity Project in Oakland, California. A self-proclaimed "theory nut," he crafted the organization's leading-for-equity framework. With collaborators Tania Anaissie, David Clifford, Tom Malarkey, and me, Cary co-created *Liberatory Design*, an approach to evolving design thinking practices with greater attention to both racial equity and complexity.

Where Do You Feel It?

Use your body as a starting point for investigating your own feelings of belonging and how you hold them in your memory.

To do this exercise, you'll need twenty minutes alone and a quiet place to sit. Close your eyes and then scan your body with your mind. Starting at your feet and moving up to the top of your head, do a mental check-in on how each part of your body feels. Ask yourself, *are there any particular parts of my body that I associate with feelings of belonging?* As you scan your body, rest your attention on each area and breathe, noting what you feel.

When students at the University of Texas, Austin, used this exercise, one recalled a time they had broken their ankle and the experience of belonging they felt when people took care of them, bringing them food and carrying their books to class. The slight soreness of their ankle when doing the body scan reminded them of how the difficult time revealed the kindness of their community.

Go slow, and give yourself grace. This exercise is not intended to trigger feelings of othering. If feelings of othering arise, breathe and relax. You don't have to dwell on anything you do not want to explore. Please take care of yourself.

Recognizing Othering

Othering is not always as explicit as a policy like apartheid, but it is often just as powerful. Othering shows up in systems like higher education, housing, and health care, which have been designed to make some people feel *less than*. It restricts the movement of whatever group is not invited in. And it refuses to let you be yourself or explore in the world as you might. The environmental cues of othering—like who is featured, who is promoted, and who can literally access a space—can belittle some, putting one identity or group above another, or disempower others based on group membership. That's what othering is. And it has devastating consequences on every level.

As you start to recognize belonging and othering, and as you learn to pay close attention to where and how they are constructed, you will begin to see how they operate both for you and for others who occupy identities and positions different from yours. A few examples of feeling othering follow. They are from different contexts to encourage you to identify where you have felt othering in play.

Being Othered at Home

I am a full-fledged adult, but when I think about a time when I didn't belong, I'm suddenly twelve again and attending my mother's second wedding. I felt extreme discomfort then. I love my stepdad and am happy he married my mother, so having such a painful feeling attached to their wedding makes me sad to this day. Looking back, I wonder what could have been different.

I can't recall how I learned that they were getting married, but I do remember having lots of questions: Was I invited? Did I have a role to play in the ceremony? That these questions still swirl in my head makes me think that attending to my sense of belonging was the furthest thing from anyone's agenda. I remember the feeling of alienation and a thought playing nonstop in my head: *Why am I here?* I was lost, not knowing what to do or who to be, almost like I was struggling to stand up straight under the weight of my confusion. Changes in my family structure triggered these feelings of not belonging.

Indeed, for many of us, our first or most poignant experiences of othering are in familial spaces. It might be feelings brought about by experiencing changes from the outside: A move, new family members, or even a shift in someone's job status from employed to unemployed can send ripples through a family unit. Or it could be happening from the inside out, when shifts in identity or willingness to disclose experiences or interests lead to feelings of alienation.

In an interview I conducted with a young woman named Sara, she mapped the ups and down of belonging in her family, recognizing that the changes in her own sexual identity caused her to feel othered in heteronormative family gatherings—the same gatherings that had previously been a source of solace and strength. She grappled with how to continue to feel close to people who were uncomfortable with changes she was making to help herself feel more authentic and whole. These tensions—both outside-in and inside-out—are some of the feelings of othering that can happen in our intimate spaces.

Being Othered in Your Community

The first day I met Heather, she cried. We were at the Stanford d.school, and Heather was apprentice coaching in one of our programs. She had come to us to explore how she might evolve her community-based work on well-being. We started talking about where we saw the work going—in what ways design could really play a role. I shared that I was building tools at the intersection of design and belonging, and she jumped right in.

As I would discover, she had come to community building after having spent time working for the US government as an intelligence analyst in counterterrorism. Heather became tearful as she told me about some of the young people she had met who had fallen victim to ISIS media units trolling for them on the internet. "The thing is," she said, "these kids are only susceptible to this outreach because they have been so consistently othered in their communities right here in the US. They have been told over and over in so many ways that they don't belong, and sadly, they start to believe it." Youth being recruited by terrorists is an extreme story, but it illustrates the potentially terrible effects of not belonging.

Othering can be extreme, but it can also be quite mundane. Small slights—not being waited on when entering a cafe, not seeing your group represented in local media, being cut off in conversation—these are all forms of othering that happen in a community on a regular basis. These actions in and of themselves might be easily dismissed, but the sting is still there, and it can accrete, building up and making one feel that belonging is not possible.

Systemic Othering

We can't talk about othering without talking about race. If you live in America today, you are likely aware of the great need to uproot systemic oppression and White supremacy culture. These come from our shared legacy of slavery, police brutality, and the interlocking forms of discrimination grounded in our collective history of racism, sexism, and capitalism. These can and do impact each of us differently, depending on our identities and experiences. What this systemic oppression looks like in your own life or communities is not always as easy to pinpoint or name as it seems to be in the movies or on the news. Complexity abounds, and that's okay. I believe we can name the bigness of the trouble we're in and also figure out ways to make progress.

There is so much social justice work to do in our communities, but often DEI work gets bogged down in a numbers game that depersonalizes the work. It can be hard to comprehend what it could mean for one's day-to-day experience to increase the percentage of people of color in leadership positions from 12 to 18 percent. Don't get me wrong; it's not that the data aren't important—they can be vital for illustrating where you are starting from and naming the scale of exclusion. Setting goals can also be highly motivating. But focusing only on numbers elides the importance and nuances of individuals' and groups' felt experience of both othering and belonging. I invite you to step into belonging as the ultimate goal in DEI work. After all, a huge part of this work is to address the feelings of othering and lack of belonging that people have every day and take steps to recognize the damage it does when allowed to fester in our systems and institutions. The work—yours and mine, along with that of other activists and allies—is to increase belonging and reduce othering in the things we build. And beyond the numbers that show progress and parity, we will know that we're getting there by the feelings people have. Not just of fitting in, but also of having a powerful seat at the table, where everyone can contribute fully and lead the way forward.

Paying attention to your own feelings will help you see the systems you are part of—including your family, community, and the larger culture—and identify where you need to design to create change. Your feelings are an antenna gathering signals and a compass that points you toward understanding and, ultimately, action.

CAMILLE FARRINGTON

Dr. Camille Farrington is managing director and senior research associate at the University of Chicago Consortium on School Research. In her book *Failing at School: Lessons for Redesigning Urban High Schools* and in her body of research, she explores belonging as a necessary component of a student's learning mindset. You can find much of her work through the Mindset Scholars Network.

Uncover Your Feelings with an Emotional Journey Map

An emotional journey map can be used to chart your feelings, both positive and negative, over time. It is used in design to help identify when and where different emotions occur. In this example, the y-axis represents the emotional ups and downs—in this case, highs and lows—of belonging, and the x-axis represents time. Use this exercise to track the emotional journey of where you live, a job you have had, or an organization of which you are a part.

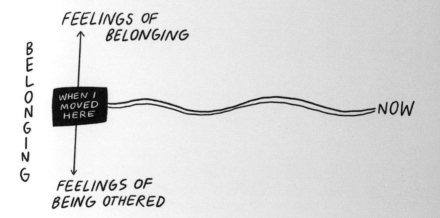

To use the journey map, think about a place where you have felt belonging or othering. Perhaps the place is the town, neighborhood, or campus where you currently live, and the time frame runs from when you originally moved there until today. Once you have a specific time and place in mind, draw a line to represent the emotional ups and downs you have experienced and make some notes about what was happening for you emotionally at those different junctures. Get as detailed as possible, exploring what circumstances created the different emotional states.

After you've made your map, reflect on what might have caused or enabled a high or low belonging experience. For the highs, was something created that supported those feelings? For the lows, did you experience explicit othering or exclusion or something more subtle?

Once you've reflected on your own experiences, use this same tool to talk to someone else about their belonging journey since joining your team or moving to your city or your country.

Why Belonging Is Important

I met Gerald at Lake Merritt in Oakland, California. The area is a kind of crossroads where people from many walks of life can be found. I go there sometimes and end up chatting with people I wouldn't otherwise meet. Gerald is an older man who had moved out of the area and was back for a visit, hanging out with his grown daughter. He said he was visiting the lake because it is one of the places he feels he belongs. It's where he and his buddies used to "make mischief." For Gerald, this area of Oakland conjures feelings of the joy and confusion of growing up and the delight of being with friends and "cruising around exploring what it was gonna be like to be on our own, out the house."

> "Human learning is socially constructed: we come to understand the world through our interactions with others. Feeling part of a community of learners is a powerful motivator."
>
> —CAMILLE FARRINGTON

Those feelings of belonging and freedom are powerful. The confidence that comes from belonging helps you try things that might be hard or scary on their own and nearly impossible without it. This sense of agency is important. In her studies of students in American high schools, Dr. Camille Farrington has shown how belonging sets up students' ability to adopt a learning mind-set, seeing themselves as learners in a school setting. This shows up particularly in students' likelihood to ask for help and use feedback to improve. Belonging is a real factor in having the confidence to believe in oneself and in one's ability to do hard things. In her book *Failing at School*, Dr. Farrington shares that when students have that sense of belonging, they "tend to interpret setbacks and difficulty in their studies as a normal part of learning, rather than as signs that they are 'out of place.'" In other words, if one can navigate (inevitable) setbacks without fear of not belonging, one has the agency to get the support needed to keep going. Research shows that better educational outcomes correlate with improved outcomes of health, wealth, and connectedness in adulthood. This means that feelings of belonging in school can have profound implications for a lifetime.

Our feelings of belonging happen in real time and space. This makes it super useful to actually ask yourself where and when you feel a sense of belonging. Social practice artist Christine Wong Yap works with people to identify where they experience belonging, the kind that lets you be brave, try new things, and work through your rough patches. As the inaugural artist-in-residence at the Haas Center for a Fair and Inclusive Society (now the Othering & Belonging Institute) at the University of California, Berkeley, Yap helped people map their places of belonging. Digging into the data she gathered, she constructed a view of some of

"Belonging happens when people feel safe, seen, and accepted."

—CHRISTINE WONG YAP

CHRISTINE WONG YAP

Christine Wong Yap is a social practice artist who has explored belonging as an aspect of psychological well-being. She has offered prompts for people to reflect on their belonging on hiking trails in Albuquerque, New Mexico, as well as in workshops with community groups in the San Francisco Bay Area. Her work in *100 Stories of Belonging in the S.F. Bay Area* inspired the Honor a Place of Belonging exercise at the end of the book.

the overlapping qualities of belonging. Well-being is the quality that is most commonly correlated with belonging, and safety, authenticity, familiarity, connectedness, access, and growth are part of it too.

The Layers of Belonging

As you dig into the concept of belonging, you may start to notice that it involves different layers: you, your identities, your group or groups, your larger communities. Belonging is not linear, nor is it usually a zero-sum game: If you feel belonging someplace or with some folks, it doesn't mean you can't feel it elsewhere too. For instance, I might belong to multiple parts of a family whose members don't all speak to each other. At the same time, I also belong to my gender, my race, the place where my ancestors came from, a work-based group, and other dimensions of my identity mostly hidden from the world. Backward and forward, my identities shape my belonging and my belonging shapes my identities. But belonging is also shaped by external factors that intersect with my identities. Structures, policies, and practices of the world all shape my experience and cue me to what parts of me I can express where. Indeed, I don't show up to work in the same way I show up to the weekly happy hour that I've been a part of for years. You too have places and situations where you show up differently depending on how you are feeling your belonging.

Locate Your Places of Belonging

Map where you feel you belong. This might be a place where you can be yourself, you feel comfortable, or you are valued. Just asking the question can be provocative. And thinking about it might reveal places where you spend a good amount of time but that don't measure up when you think about your sense of belonging.

Sketch out a rough map of a place or places you occupy: your home, school campus, gym, office, volunteer organization, town, state. The location you map could be big or small, and your map could be a loose sketch of boxes or bubbles, a printout of a map, or an actual road map. Identify where you feel a sense of belonging. Perhaps these are the places where you feel seen or where your voice matters. They could also be the places where your bodily needs are seamlessly attended to or your contribution is valued.

Take time to reflect on each location and what it feels like there.

bell hooks

bell hooks is a writer and cultural critic known for her contributions to feminist theory and cultural studies. She has written many books that explore community and resistance to patriarchy, White supremacy, and capitalism. *Belonging: A Culture of Place* is a collection of essays based on her return to Kentucky, where she teaches at Berea College.

No one is alone in the world. This process of reading cues for when, where, and how we can belong happens for you and for every other individual and the groups and communities we all belong to at the same time. As humans, we instinctively pay attention to whose belonging is being supported and whose is not in order to minimize damage from othering.

"Currently in our nation Americans of all colors feel bereft of a sense of 'belonging' to either a place or a community. Yet most people still long for community and that yearning is a place of possibility, the place where we might begin as a nation to think and dream anew about the building of beloved community."

—bell hooks

In her essay collection *Belonging,* writer and activist bell hooks speaks to what belonging feels like across a time and place. She discusses her home state of Kentucky, where she has resettled after a long time away, describing the hills, "the rich Kentucky soil," playing in the dirt as a child, and her grandfather's bountiful crops. She also talks about what she sees now: the ongoing need to end racial oppression and heal the earth. As she literally speaks of the dirt, she unearths what can be described as the architecture of belonging. It is composed of so many elements: people, land, history, a legacy of racial segregation. Time away helped hooks see these pieces;

she chooses to reclaim them and work for needed change. In a sense, she chooses to *belong* to the layers of her experience—to the place, the people, and the complexities of identity—and to work to disrupt oppression in myriad forms.

Her unearthing of these layers—some delightful, some painful—is an invitation to design by investigating what is happening around you, to interrogate what is going on and use that effort to see not just what is in front of you but also what is below the surface. Who has been erased? Who has been promoted? What harms continue? Her essay collection is a sparkling exemplar of how to see what is happening in one's own context. To build belonging and reduce othering in your context will also require this kind of excavation. You can explore the layers of your own feelings in the next exercise. And in the next part, you will be guided to look more closely at the moments where belonging and othering happen.

Metaphors

Design professor Tom Maiorana and I explored some of the meanings of belonging for our Placemaking Project, which was sponsored by the University of California, Davis, and aimed at using art and design to connect people and place. To engage people, we stenciled fill-in-the-blank prompts with biodegradable spray paint on the sidewalk in a busy public area and offered chalk for passersby to fill in their answers.

As people completed their own metaphors, we talked to them about their feelings of belonging. We were struck by how interested folks were in talking about belonging and also by how much they saw their city as a place they could belong. The idea of family came up a lot, as did the freedom to be yourself. One woman wrote, "Belonging in Oakland is like a tree because we are all connected." Another chalked, "Belonging in Oakland is like family because we keep ascending"; her friend beside her added, "Belonging in Oakland is like a whirlwind because you never know what direction the wind is blowing."

It can be useful to create your own metaphors as a way to get in touch with your feelings of belonging: when and where you have them and what they look like. Is there a metaphor to describe how belonging looks for you?

Fill in the blanks here to come up with your own metaphors of belonging and othering. You might try this multiple times or with friends, colleagues, or strangers to spark a conversation about belonging, othering, and the differences between them.

Belonging is like _____ because _____ .
Belonging looks like _____ because _____ .
Belonging feels like _____ because _____ .

Othering is like _____ because _____ .
Othering looks like _____ because _____ .
Othering feels like _____ because _____ .

Culture is built every day in the behaviors of a group and in the meanings that accumulate from them. A culture of belonging happens when no one is explicitly watching, on days when there isn't a special meeting to work on it. Examples of belonging are:

- Picking up a piece of trash so wheelchair access is not obstructed.
- Asking everyone to introduce themselves and ensuring that all voices are heard.
- Avoiding esoteric acronyms when they aren't necessary.
- Using the pronouns that people prefer, and sharing your own, if and when you are ready.
- Showing respect through actions that support everyone to be their best selves.
- Honoring each other's contributions.

To change culture, then, is about everyday acts. This means you can start small, try lots of things, and see what works. Not because your aspirations are small, but because this gives you the opportunity to tune yourself to see, feel, and notice what is changing, how it's changing, and for whom. Noticing what is working and for whom, who belongs and who doesn't, and when and under what circumstances gets you ready to design to change culture, to craft everyday acts of intentional design toward belonging and away from othering.

Code Switching: This can be a nuanced moment of moving between aspects of identity.

Contributing: Perhaps the holy grail, contributing is also a circle—the more you belong, the more you can contribute; the more you contribute, likely the more you belong.

Flowing: Feeling the rhythm and the dance of the group or your role within it.

Dissenting: No community can thrive without understanding how to work with conflict and disagreement.

Repairing: Hurt happens; how you recover from it is a profound indicator of belonging.

Diverging and Exiting: What feelings should exist for those who leave and those who stay behind?

Even if you weren't explicitly aware of these as design moments, you have likely already intentionally designed some of them. Right now, as you read about each moment, direct your attention to identifying and then feeling into the moments that you have to work with in your program, organization, or gathering. Which moments have you already thought about? Which have you not yet considered? Each one has different possibilities that are worth noticing and exploring. Pay attention to which ones are provocative, and ask yourself why.

In the pages that follow, I discuss each moment and offer lots of questions for you to consider. You might want to jot down what the questions get you thinking about. This will be good fodder for the last part, where you will be prompted to design the moments that matter most in your community. If you are feeling antsy, that's a feeling too; perhaps you can push yourself to notice and inquire more.

The Invitation

Belonging begins with an invitation into a space. How one is invited matters a lot. Whether the invitation to your group comes personally from a friend or anonymously as a notice on a hallway bulletin board, the invitation is the first opportunity to create a moment of belonging.

This moment is so obvious and so important. You can probably think of a time when the way you were invited in made you feel special and another time when it filled you with confusion or doubt—like it did for me at my mom's wedding, way back when. To be the uninvited guest, interloper, or intruder can feel powerful if the interruption is purposeful, but feeling that way when you've actually been invited is the worst.

To see this important moment in action, take a look at the invitation offered to the world by you or your organization. It could be a literal invitation sent via mail or an evite sent as a blast. It might also be the facade of your space, an ambassador out in the field, or your website and other media assets. Broadly speaking, the invitation is the first encounter someone has with you, your team, the way your organization thinks, even your values. While the specifics may vary widely, when you are seeking to understand how your invitation exists out in the world, consider some key attributes:

- Who does it come from?
- How findable is it?
- Does it require prior knowledge to understand?
- Does it require specific technologies to view it?
- Is access restricted in any way?

A great invitation speaks to your audience with a clear purpose. Focus on the feeling you want people to have when learning of the invitation and glimpsing your values. If you want it to feel warm, does that mean the all-encompassing embrace of a bear hug or the inviting glimmer of a candle across a room?

Invitations also matter for pattern breaking. If you're hoping to move beyond your existing community, you can't rely on your old email list or regular outreach channels. When you are trying to mix things up, intentionality is critical. It is critical to be clear about who you seek to engage and to understand why they may not have been—or have not _felt_ they were—invited before. Recognize the history of how different groups have been invited, and address those

"It is revolutionary for any trans person to choose to be seen and visible in a world that tells us we should not exist."

—LAVERNE COX

practices directly. If you're ready to try something new, playing with how you invite people is super ripe for experimentation. Try an A/B test: Use one invitation and see who shows. Then use another version and see if a different crew arrives.

Trans actress Laverne Cox offers a fierce reminder that being able to show up as yourself, the *you* that you want to be, is a critical piece of belonging. Environments that invite people in, then create and celebrate opportunities for those people to be their full selves, are foundational to belonging in any community. In her advocacy work, Cox illuminates the interdependence of visibility and authenticity. As she has said, "We are not what other people say we are. We are who we know ourselves to be, and we are what we love." This is a call to leave room for everyone to be who they want to be.

Keep expanding your thinking about what an invitation is. Sometimes the way we behave acts as an invitation for others to do the same. Let your actions be an invitation to others to be themselves in all of their glory.

Notice

- What surprising invitations have you received that unlocked belonging for you?
- How do you invite people into your space or program?
- Who is your welcoming for, and who might not feel so welcome?
- How might you invite difference (different people, different behaviors, different responses) into your work and your life?
- How do your actions work as an invitation for others to show up as themselves?

Investigate Your Invitation

Take a look at your invitation as it exists right now. It might be a literal invitation or a way of understanding your first point of contact with someone you'd like to join you in your work or play as a new customer, guest, or collaborator.

Once you have identified what your moment of invitation is, consider this set of qualities and ask yourself where your invitation falls on these continuums: Is it more mysterious or clear? Does it require high tech, or is it low tech? Not all of these qualities will be relevant, and that's okay. Use the ones that matter most to you.

Clear	←——→	Mysterious
Public	←——→	Private
Open	←——→	Closed
Accessible	←——→	Inaccessible
Widely announced	←——→	Word of mouth
Large-scale	←——→	Intimate
High-tech	←——→	Low-tech
Prior knowledge	←——→	Show up as a novice

After you have plotted where your invitation sits along these continuums, what do you notice? Are there any surprises? Do you see qualities that you want to shift one way or the other?

After you've done your own reflection, ask someone who has received your invitation to give you feedback. Your inquiry will help you see how your invitation is functioning for others. And if you need to improve it, you've got some emergent metrics to help you gauge progress.

LAVERNE COX

Laverne Cox is a trans actress and activist. Her breakthrough role was as Sophia Burset in the television series *Orange Is the New Black*, and she has since been an important spokesperson for the human rights of trans people. As a producer of *Disclosure: Trans Lives on Screen,* she explores the damaging legacy of trans representation in cinema and her hopes for the future.

Entering

In workshops she hosts at the d.school, dancer and professor Aleta Hayes begins with what she calls a threshold exercise. She builds a makeshift doorway to the school's large atrium space and stops the whole class before they can enter. Pointing out the existence of this threshold, Hayes instructs the students that when they step across it they must let the music move them into the space beyond. Her insistence that how one enters a space is a profound moment of design has always struck me as gold.

> "Dancing your way in is powerful. It's you entering the collective space. Do it your way."
>
> —ALETA HAYES

Hayes's work is deeply about design, profoundly about belonging, and fully embodied in dance. The way she uses dance gives us the chance to remember that experiences happen in our bodies. With her threshold exercise she illuminates a passage; in doing so, she shines a light not just on dance, but also on *experience design:* that push to craft an experience we can feel and remember in our bodies.

As Hayes illustrates, how you come into a space and the kind of entrance you create for others matters on a number of fronts. Examining how people join your space—literally or figuratively—offers up tremendous opportunities to reflect on belonging.

Kat Holmes, author of *Mismatch: How Inclusion Shapes Design*, reminds us that, "An inclusive environment is far more than the shape of its doors, chairs, and rampways. It also considers the psychological and emotional impact on people." Think about the differences you feel when entering a cathedral, a dive bar, an amusement park, or an online gaming environment. The architecture of the entrance, or the process of going in, directly impacts a whole range of feelings, and belonging is very likely among them. Because the entry creates a first impression and sets a tone, it's important to put belonging at the forefront of the experience. This is precisely why Walmart has stationed greeters right inside their front doors and why fancy hotels open onto lounges.

ALETA HAYES

Aleta Hayes is a dancer, choreographer, and teacher.
She is a lecturer in the Department of Dance at Stanford
University and a frequent contributor to d.school
workshops. In her teaching, she creates a space where
even those who don't see themselves as dancers connect
with their own movement abilities as part of building
their creative confidence.

Beyond the physical entry to a space, also consider what actions are required upon entry. Is there a verbal greeting, a bow, a place to sign in? Must badges or visitor passes be obtained from a front desk? Maybe there's a costume change, as when doctors and nurses envelop themselves in personal protective equipment to enter a quarantine ward or the operating room. People may enter a building, a set of practices, or even an identity.

Entering sets the stage for participation to follow. If it is your first year of college or a job interview, you could be feeling quite anxious. The entry can cue you as to the best way to participate so you can relax into your reasons for being there. If it doesn't, you may face an uncertain path toward understanding the role you can play. Confusion at the entry point can set people up to feel othered.

Entering a space also means entering the story of that space—the characters, the rules, and the history are part of the environment. For the person who doesn't know the full story, navigating an entrance for the first time can be either tantalizing or scary.

You can get to know the sensations participants are likely to have when they enter your space or organization by shadowing them—with their consent, of course! For example, when Scott Cook was developing the accounting software Quicken (a precursor to QuickBooks), he famously waited outside of computer stores and asked people if he could watch them install the software in their home. As a result, he got to witness firsthand the feelings and frustrations of the customers' entry journey while they installed the software, learning far more than if he had just asked them about it. This honest and open approach to developing a better understanding of his customers' needs helped Cook grow one piece of software into the personal finance giant Intuit.

 Notice

- What happens when you enter a public space? The next time you enter a restaurant, store, office, or health care facility, pay attention. What feelings do you have? How was the space crafted for you to enter?

- What is it about the experience of entering a space that cues you for how to belong? Which details shape your experience, and how do they set you up to participate?

- How do you set up others to enter your space—physical, digital, or organizational?

- How can you help people enter a space in a way that sets the right tone for the activity inside?

- Pay attention to patterns. Do people of particular backgrounds feel invited in, but then stumble at the entry? Follow up to understand who feels they can join the story and who does not.

Stop and Linger at the Entry . . .

We can be in such a rush to get to wherever we are going that we completely miss the entry and all the belonging clues it offers. This exercise is a reminder to stop and linger at the entry. It could be the grocery store, the airport, a high-end boutique. Perhaps it is a literal border crossing between towns or even between countries. Wherever the entry is, stop and sketch it, making a flow chart of the steps in the process. Then go back and experience it again. In your second time through, identify what is happening in:

- **The built environment:** Are there physical barriers, doorways, or open flows?
- **The visual plane:** What's the role of signage? Is media being served to you?
- **Person-to-person interactions:** Is someone there to greet you or check your credentials?

When and where within the entry process do you feel belonging or not, and how was that constructed?

You can invite others to try this too, then compare your experiences.

Participating

You've been invited, you've entered, and here you are. Ta-da! As a moment in a belonging journey, participation is the heart of the matter. The meat of it. Presumably the best part of belonging is full participation. That definition might make it hard to read participation as a moment, but let's try.

The ways in which participation occurs vary widely, and the moments you have experienced might look very different from someone else's. Participation could be a full day at Disneyland, a deep and philosophical conversation between a mentor and mentee, or years of service as an employee or volunteer. While the scale of the participation may be different, essentially it's about knowing that your being there in the mix actually matters.

My long-ago colleague and friend Peter used to work on Capitol Hill. As the constituent liaison for a congressperson, he took care of all the correspondence between the elected official and the folks back home. It was pretty grueling, involving tons of research and writing, but he was helping people participate in democracy. The letters, emails, and phone calls he oversaw put people in touch with their government in a concrete way. His work showed the constituents that their inquiries mattered and they were indeed participating in a civic process. Peter's attention also functioned as a kind of encouragement for the people to keep going and do more in their communities by showing up to hearings and congressional town halls. Peter was always looking for ways to let the district's constituents know they were part of something and they belonged, whether their views were in line with or opposed to the congressperson's.

The moment of participation is sometimes where othering shows up, in both subtle and explicit ways. Did you ever get fired up for an event at school only to arrive and feel like it was executed for younger kids? Or show up to a workout class and realize that it required specialized equipment you didn't have? It's a buzzkill, at a minimum, and it can engender feelings of othering, especially in folks who are vulnerable.

For participation to be centered in belonging, paying attention really matters. Hannah Joy Root, the d.school's community manager, experienced this when hosting Durell Coleman's Design the Future program. His program engaged students not currently living with physical disabilities to design with community members who use wheelchairs and other assistive devices. On a day when the whole crew was coming to the d.school to do some prototyping, she noticed that all the prototyping tables were too high for the designers in wheelchairs. She moved quickly to modify the tables so they were the appropriate height. Having learned from the experience, she made sure that even after the program there were always tables at different heights in the studio.

Getting to full participation requires attention to many details, from checking in to inquire explicitly how people are doing to inviting reflection and feedback on how it feels to be part of the work or organization. This kind of awareness, attention, and support is built into any adept leader's approach, and it becomes especially important for building belonging. Participating can be a time of interconnection between the various moments we experience in our communities: the work that has been done to invite people in, ensure a powerful entry experience, and encourage authentic contributions. These moments either pay dividends as full participation or reveal some of the feelings that undermine it.

Notice

- What are the mechanisms for authentic participation in your group or place? How does participation happen, and what makes it feel good?
- What does it mean to take up a new identity when you join a new crew and begin to participate fully?

Code Switching

We rarely speak in precisely the same way everywhere we go. Whether we're at home, at work, or playing a pickup game of ball with friends, we likely have different ways of talking for each situation. The process of switching between languages in this way is called "code switching." While it can refer to switching between two completely different languages—English and Spanish, for example— code switching is more commonly used to refer to switching between vernaculars, and it is a marker of being part of more than one culture.

The concept was pulled from linguistics into broader use as a way to understand the relationships between White dominant culture and other, nondominant cultures. And it often indicates an authentic ability to stand apart from dominant cultural norms or to move fluidly between cultures. Code switching is an incredible skill of adaptation and an ability to move fluidly between contexts, and it can also entail a cognitive load that can be draining.

A perfect and entertaining example of code switching is embedded in Boots Riley's film *Sorry to Bother You*. In the movie, new telemarketer Cassius Green struggles to get people to stay on the phone, until his experienced colleague, Langston, teaches him to use his "White voice." In his instruction, Langston tells Cassius, "No. You got it wrong. It's not about sounding all nasal. It's about sounding like you don't have a care. Like your bills are paid and you're happy about your future and you're about to jump in your Ferrari when you get off this call." As a result of Langston's advice, Cassius's sales go gangbusters, but using this new skill to become a star salesperson ends up drawing him into a surreal corporate conspiracy. Riley's work is both over the top and nuanced and a brilliant representation of code switching (as well as a critique of capitalist culture run amok).

> "I try to find creative ways to put ideas out to make the ground fertile for organizers."
>
> —BOOTS RILEY

BOOTS RILEY

Boots Riley is a musician and filmmaker based in Oakland, California. His film *Sorry to Bother You* was both critically acclaimed and a contribution to a conversation about the experience of Black Americans in late capitalism. You can watch the film again and again to experience layers of othering and belonging.

In our pluralistic world, the goal is not to eliminate code switching, but rather to understand when, where, and, especially, for whom it is at play. As a moment of belonging, code switching can be both a powerful resource and an added weight to bear, and it is likely experienced as both at different times. Learning to pay attention to code switching and its assets, especially for those people who are primarily identified with the dominant culture, is an important way to ensure that all community members are able to fully contribute and belong.

You can often notice code switching when contexts shift. Teachers can observe the shift in students from the classroom to the playground and back again. As kids leave a classroom, they can drop their academic English and slip into potentially more comfortable ways of communicating with their peers and friends. In super diverse schools, a unique mélange sometimes develops as kids learn and use each other's vernaculars. In work environments, the shift might happen on the journey from the break room to the board room or in the move from talking among team members to talking to clients or customers.

By seeking to notice and understand code switching in your community, you effectively give voice to the many groups and subgroups that are part of people's identities. This is a huge win for belonging. In fact, the skills embedded in code switching can also be cause for acknowledgment and celebration. I recently heard a leader say to a teammate, "Thank you for speaking so openly with our new participant. I could tell he felt really seen when you spoke with him."

Code switching is part of authentic communication, and it deserves to be honored.

And when the effort appears taxing for people in your community, you can design to lighten the load by diversifying your team and ensuring that multiple codes are in play. If you know that you code switch yourself, you can show your crew that you can handle more than the dominant cultural norms. Just watch out for appropriation or overly performative connections. Tuning into code switching as a moment of belonging is really about listening for understanding. It is listening for how language is a cue for belonging—and for whom. You have to tune your listening to understand whether you are welcome or not.

Notice

- When and where do you experience code switching, either in yourself or in others?

- If you know you code switch, what feelings do you have about it? If you don't think you ever code switch, what does that make you think?

- Have you found code switching to be taxing, liberating, or both for yourself or others?

Listen for It

Make tomorrow your day to listen for code switching and how it is or isn't present in your context. Then go further and listen for other forms of belonging and othering. Grab a journal and pause frequently to write down things you've heard—in a meeting, on a video call, on the news, during a podcast, or from a radio personality. You will be surprised by what you notice in just ten minutes of intentional listening or a day's worth of keeping an ear open with this idea in mind.

At the end of the day, consider the following questions:

- Did you notice any code switching or other contextual adjustments that people made?
- What did you hear that reminded you of any of the moments of belonging—like inviting, contributing, dissenting?
- When did you hear language that seemed to be othering a group or individual? How or why was that happening?

Contributing

In my interviews with a wide range of people about belonging, many said they knew they belonged to whatever community they were part of when they felt they were making a contribution. A friend who was a visiting scholar at a university knew she belonged when she was able to introduce two coworkers to each other. Her presence allowed it to happen, and she knew then that she had made a contribution to the campus and to her colleagues' work together. In another example, my colleague Jorge showed up to drop off his kid at soccer and ended up staying for the whole practice because the coach really needed an extra adult to run the young players through their drills. That's a form of contributing that arises only when a sense of belonging is in place, and it builds on itself.

Contributing can take so many forms. Through your being: your presence and words. Through your expressions: your talents, advocacy, anger, humor, and joy. Through your actions: by making connections, bringing food, caring for others, or showing up. In short, being you. As simple as that sounds, it is not always easy. You might be nervous or, having been othered elsewhere, unclear how to show up. In many contexts people honestly don't know what they are bringing to the table, or they may be shy to share authentically.

For the moment of contributing to sing with belonging, often we need to actively cultivate it through reflection. When my friend Amanda was the principal at a brand-new school, she organized professional learning days for her staff so they could learn not only what they needed for the year ahead, but also about each other. She knew that if she gave staff the chance to reflect on what they were bringing to the community as it was being formed, they would more readily contribute and that would build their sense of belonging. Since the curriculum was intended to integrate the arts, Amanda began each day of the two-week intensive before school started by asking the newly hired teachers to share an artistic practice they enjoy. Not all the teachers were artists or musicians, but they each brought something to share that showcased who they are and introduced their approach to teaching.

Amanda was leading with what author and consultant Peter Block considers one of the key ways to build belonging in community-based work: the sharing of our gifts. Like the set of moments that I have offered in this

> "Belonging occurs when we tell others what gift we receive from them."

—PETER BLOCK

chapter, Block envisions six key "conversations," as he calls them, that are critical for building belonging: invitation, possibility, ownership, dissent, commitment, and gifts. *Gifts* is the sixth and last conversation because by then the stage has been set for people to offer themselves. While giving the gift is important, it is equally or even more important to know that it has been received and that you are seen.

People's contributions—big and small—matter. And you can design opportunities for people to recognize and share their gifts. When the stage is set for contribution, a kind of flow can begin. This is why design can be so important. First learn about your own gifts through self-reflection and feedback, then explore how to offer more of yourself. It's part of a leader's role to ensure space for everyone's gifts to be shared as well as a balance between contributing and self-care.

Notice

- Where do you contribute, and how does it shape your belonging?
- What opportunities do people in your group have to share their gifts and make meaningful contributions?
- Do you need to create new opportunities for people to share their gifts and know that their contributions matter?
- How does any given moment of contribution have ripple effects?

PETER BLOCK

Peter Block is an author and organizational development consultant based in Cincinnati, Ohio. His book *Community: The Structure of Belonging* is a source of inspiration for community-based facilitators across the country.

Flowing

Coined by psychologist Mihaly Csikszentmihalyi, *flow* is a term for the state of being that comes from full immersion in the task at hand. For some, it comes from dance or play, both literally and figuratively. In community, it can be the outgrowth of belonging. And unfortunately flow is not always achieved. Implicit or explicit othering can be what prevents an individual or a group from getting into flow.

The ability to play together is a powerful sign of a group getting into flow and potentially building belonging. At Playworks, a national nonprofit dedicated to ensuring that all kids have access to healthy play, founder Jill Vialet said to me, "Play contributes directly to a person's ability to handle failure, work in teams, and take risks." Whether it is an outdoor game among kids, a board game among adults, or a full-throttle race around the playground, the ebbs and flows of play enliven people and let them show up in new ways. Collaborative structures—like turn taking and high-fiving with a "good job, nice try" instead of ridiculing foul-ups—support working together. As you are noticing play in your home or office or at the playground near you, tune in to the rhythms you see and hear. They may remind you of what flow feels like.

Pay attention to how flow is helping to build belonging and vice versa. Flow can be a notable, nearly palpable moment to look for in your event, community, or environment. You'll recognize that your group is in flow when getting to work feels authentic and deep; when conversation matters; when hurdles are hard, but surmountable. For my colleague Joaquin, flow happens when his whole community shows for the neighborhood cleanup. For Davida, a health care worker I interviewed, it's when she is able to meet each new patient at the clinic door and walk them in to their appointment so she knows they are being cared for by the team.

When you are in flow, you're not wasting resources on wondering if you are part of the community; instead, you know you are. For some, flow is in and of itself a measure of belonging. You can't achieve it unless everyone has a solid understanding and command of their role and can hand off their cares to the next person as needed.

Flow rarely happens without commingling with authentic purpose. Think of a dedicated emergency room doctor or a translator working overseas—the work is exhausting, but they have purpose and are moved to serve. You might notice that you feel more belonging when you are centered on your purpose, collaborating with others, or focused on a goal. Some signs that point to flow include the hum of chitchat while working, laughter coming from a discussion group, and the ability to accomplish goals without extra stress. When you see it and feel it, work to notice what helped it happen. If belonging was created, you've likely got something valuable to build upon.

 Notice

- When and where are the people you work with, the patients you serve, the kids you wrangle, or the executives you coach in flow?
- When and where do you feel flow?
- When and where does your sense of belonging intersect with feelings of flow?

Dissenting

No community can thrive without understanding how to work with dissent. Communicating dissent can be real evidence that you trust in your community. Isn't the way a group deals with disagreements a measure of belonging? You are likely to raise issues, challenge authority, or push beyond the status quo only if you have a sense of belonging. And if you are othered for raising issues, it is likely the group needs to dig more deeply into supporting differing opinions and how they can be productive. Without dissent, mistrust, disgust, and despair can arise. If people can't express a grievance or share a disruptive idea, they might as well not be there. When that's the case, you can feel it. Belonging appears to be present only on the surface, and that feeling tends to limit the whole community's growth.

At the University of California, Berkeley, the director of the Othering & Belonging Institute, john a. powell, supports the idea that full belonging means having the right to make demands. You can ask for what you need *and* influence the system. This freedom is a profound measure of belonging: I know I belong when I can advocate for myself and for others.

"Belonging means more than just being seen. Belonging entails having a meaningful voice and the opportunity to participate in the design of social and cultural structures. Belonging means having the right to contribute to and make demands on society and political institutions."

—john a. powell

Take some time to consider how people make demands, express discontent, and dissent. You can actively encourage and shape these abilities through design; the work can also move beyond individual groups and organizations to encompass the larger systems to which we belong: Demand the right to a powerful education. Demand an end to police brutality. Demand a living wage. Demand housing for all.

Consider this story from Cori about the homeless services center where she used to

john a. powell

john a. powell is the director of the Othering & Belonging
Institute at the University of California, Berkeley. He
writes and speaks widely about bridging as a way to
create the beloved community we wish to see in our
world. He coauthored *The Problem of Othering: Towards
Inclusiveness and Belonging* with Stephen Menendian.

spend her winter nights. The rule at the center was that the youth experiencing homelessness had to be outside of the center for at least half of the day. On one particular evening, the temperature was well below freezing in her Midwestern town, so Cori told her friends she wasn't going to leave in the morning. They looked bewildered, but when the time came, they joined her, and so did the staff. Nobody left the center to go out into the cold. Shortly after the protest, the center canceled the policy and offered round-the-clock shelter. Cori has her own apartment now, but it's this moment of dissent, leading a spontaneous rebellion, that she remembers when she thinks about belonging. It is the kind of belonging that came from finding her voice; as she says, "I knew I did something important by standing up."

Brené Brown is a research professor and author. Her notion of "true belonging" has put belonging on the map for many. For Brown, true belonging means you carry your belonging with you. It is resilience and self-compassion—not merely fitting in. Brown calls for true belonging to be a north star and letting that sense of being who you are lead you. It's the kind of belonging that gives you the confidence to stand alone when you must.

According to Brown, in a world rife with divisions, stepping into conversation with people different from oneself is hard and increasingly rare. She encourages us to see that we can all find belonging in ourselves and use that to be in relationship with those who don't look, talk, or act like us. We can do our own work to collaborate with others in new ways.

Your own work might be healing or sharing your discontent. Or perhaps it's more time alone to build reserves or more dedication to moving beyond old or inherited dynamics.

Brown does not use design as her frame for making change, and yet in her book *Braving the Wilderness* she writes of her push to "create cultures where people feel safe—where their belonging is not threatened by speaking out and they are supported when they make the decision to brave the wilderness, stand alone, and speak truth to bullshit." Speaking truth to bullshit is not easy. Sometimes that means saying what needs to be said, even though it might be out of turn. It is, however, an invitation for design to shape the journey, craft new interactions, confront what doesn't work, and host the conversations you want or need to have.

"True belonging is the spiritual practice of believing in and belonging to yourself so deeply that you can share your most authentic self with the world and find sacredness in both being a part of something and standing alone in the wilderness."

—BRENÉ BROWN

BRENÉ BROWN

Dr. Brené Brown is a social worker by training, a professor by occupation, and a writer, speaker, and thought leader by vocation. Of her multiple best-selling books, *Braving the Wilderness* is the one to read if you want her take on belonging. She defines and shares stories about the phenomenon she calls "true belonging."

When I asked my friend Jess to talk about a time he felt othered, he did not hesitate. It was while he was in the Coast Guard. Although he had found a warm sense of belonging starting with his time at the academy and he made good friends and always felt he was doing important work as an officer, he can pinpoint two very specific times when he felt the horrible and, in his words, the "prickly" feeling of othering. The first instance was when a commanding officer said disparaging things about Mexican immigrants, calling them dangerous criminals. As the grandson of a Mexican immigrant, this did not sit well with him. Jess said, "I am so proud of my grandfather and the family he built after coming to the United States. It was hard to hear him make a blanket statement that I knew was untrue and to think that others were accepting it because it came from the commanding officer." The second experience was when a senior officer spoke ill of the Somali refugee community. Again, Jess had had a different experience. He had tutored young Somali kids at the library and knew that they and their families had been invited here, having escaped a devastating war. In both cases, Jess still wishes that he had been able to offer a different point of view and that the othering comments could have at the very least been shown to be part of a complex story—one in which not all immigrants and refugees are branded as criminals. He fears that these types of "sound bites can lodge in people's minds and be dangerous or, at least, certainly not our best."

Taking up dissent as a moment of design can be super useful. Doing it in advance, before any problems arise, is perhaps more enlightened than many people or organizations will manage, but you can still attend to it authentically and compassionately when it emerges.

 Notice

- When was a time you wish you had spoken up? And what enables you to be brave in your home, workplace, or community?

- In what ways do you use dissent productively?

- Can your group hold differing opinions of varying sizes or levels of concern without othering?

- What would it look like to build in more opportunities to hear and learn from dissenting views?

Assumption Storm

This classic design exercise is often used at the start
of innovation projects to identify fertile terrain for
change. Here you can use the method to see into your
context in new ways and explore what is and isn't
supporting belonging.

An assumption storm requires three steps. You can do
this on your own or with a team.

1. Generate all the assumptions you have about who belongs
   and why.
2. Consciously seek to flip those assumptions by coming up
   with all the possible opposites.
3. Brainstorm ways to achieve your flips using different design
   levers (see page 84).

An afterschool program coordinator I worked with did an
assumptions storm with her team to identify who they
were serving well and who they were not. After listing
a wide range of assumptions, they realized that they
implicitly felt the kids who were officially enrolled in their
program belonged, but their friends—who sometimes
came along—were often othered, made to wait in the hall
or told to come back later. The assumption that "tagalong"
friends did not belong jumped out, and they decided to flip
that assumption and ask themselves what they could do
to include those friends. Ideas included hosting a bring-a-
friend day, creating a specific time for friends to drop in, or
having a flyer ready for kids to take home to their parents
to consider enrolling them.

Repairing

I had a teeny tiny wedding. Honestly, it wasn't how I had imagined it, but my partner knew he didn't want to meet people for the first time on such an intimate occasion. It felt important to honor his wish, and to this day I love his self-knowledge. So, instead of a hundred people, we invited our parents and siblings and six friends each. I did not make a list and cut people. That would have been too painful. But it turned out that, in addition to my best friend from high school, everyone I invited had been a roommate of mine. When I realized that, I felt comfortable with the decision, but I wasn't sure how to tell my other besties that I would not be including them. I just said it was going to be a small, family wedding. That was a version of the truth, but not quite the whole truth.

Fast forward sixteen years, and I suddenly realized that a good friend of mine had no idea that other friends had been at my wedding. It felt crappy, and I needed to own up to my elision. I recognized this as a moment of repair. So I called her up and said something like, "Hey, I am practicing repair and wanted to share something with you that happened. I am afraid it might be hurtful, but I think telling you about it might prevent hurt further down the road." Yup, it was super awkward. She said it was odd because it did hurt, but she was glad to know, and she agreed that finding out accidentally would have been worse. I think she appreciated that I made the effort. It was also helpful that we named it as a moment: the moment of repair.

Clearly this moment is not always as simple as a phone call, or we would have much less hurt in our world. Repair is part of the bridge from othering to belonging. Depending on the circumstances, it could take a generation or more, operating at scales from the intimate to the systemic to achieve repair. And like all the moments of belonging, seeing it and naming it are critical first steps. If we recognize that repair is needed, it becomes available to design.

Nikole Hannah-Jones, one of the great American speakers and writers on reparations for slavery in our time, opened her recent *New York Times Magazine* piece by saying, "If true justice and equality are ever to be achieved in the United States, the country must finally take seriously what it owes black Americans." Indeed. Her statement makes me wonder what we can design to make it possible to heed her call. To be clear, I am in no way equating my lingering sadness about a wedding invite with the need to recover from the legacy of slavery in our country. Rather, I am saying that in order to recover from most things—from the trivial to the traumatic—we have to pause for a moment of repair. This is why, for instance, South Africa's Truth and Reconciliation process was so powerful and there are renewed calls for reparations for slavery here in the United States. Depending on the situation, repair could take years of creative work and a kind of tenacity not always apparent in our national culture, or it could be a simple phone call, but healing of any kind surely won't happen without recognizing the need to repair what has been broken.

 Notice

- Do you have experience with repair? How did it operate? What did it feel like?

- Are you holding onto something that needs repair?

- How could a focus on belonging support reparations?

Diverging and Exiting

For years I designed learning experiences with precise start times, I shared the agenda with participants ahead of time, and I built wiggle room into the schedule in case things got off track. Still, people arrived late or had to leave early. I don't think of myself as a control freak, but it would kind of rattle me. One day my mentor and friend Mark Salinas at the National Equity Project showed me that he always makes space for folks to speak to what he calls "comings and goings," a way to give voice to the schedule modifications that are part of any gathering, no matter how intentionally it was designed. Today I think of the comings and goings as a simple truth of nearly all communities: If we are building true belonging into the group, we will always be accommodating diverging paths. And that's not a bad thing; it's a sign of a living and breathing organization.

I recently received a text message from a friend that said: "On Friday I have a conflicting invite and while I LOVE your group and my belonging in it, I may choose this less-often-available opportunity, knowing my belonging in your regular Friday cocktail persists." It made me realize that belonging *somewhere* can be a helpful driver for doing other things; for example, exploring a boundary, stretching, taking a risk, coming and going. The group in which we feel belonging has our back; it's saying: *You got this. You do you. You can belong here even when you explore other things.*

Our opportunity is to design for both convergence and divergence, to embrace the ebbs and flows, and to use design to invite the outcomes of engaged pluralism. We stop and start at different times. We learn at different paces. We hold different beliefs. Whether it is a gap-year program, a work-trade arrangement, or reentry after incarceration, design can help build the paths and lanes, the on- and off-ramps that people need to be part of a greater whole.

To successfully design for diverging paths, you can go broad and seek an audience that is truly diverse in its needs. Having different kinds of people at different stages of their lives in your organization will invariably push you to create more paths. You can also help people visualize their needs—mapping what journeys are possible and inventing new pathways as needed. And finally, you can design for endings with as much intention as you design the invitation.

Indeed, let's not forget exits. People leave. It happens. Consider how it should feel to exit—for those who leave and for those who stay behind. While it might feel easier to design a welcome, perhaps a departure or return is just as important as a moment of belonging.

Notice

- What do comings and goings within your community feel like?
- When and where are there opportunities to accommodate and embrace diverging paths?
- What does it feel like to contemplate designing for an exit?

More Moments

At the start of this chapter is a beautiful mural featuring nine moments of belonging. They are great places to start, but there are many more possible moments. Now that you have an awareness of how to see belonging, what other moments can you name? Other ways to describe some of the moments I've worked with include the welcome, celebration, full community, making demands, the dance, reflection, and gratitude. I've heard others use outreach, initiation, seeking, onboarding, on-ramp, off-ramp, check-in, and checkout. Seeing and identifying the moments where people could experience belonging is your invitation to shape them. Continue to identify the moments you can design for, and broaden the spaces where you can build belonging.

With these moments in mind, it's time to explicitly design for belonging. You could choose to work with any of the nine moments we just explored together or any others that emerged as particularly relevant in your context. You might even find that you have some pent-up energy or heat around a particular moment and are primed to make change happen. That's awesome. Keep that charge in mind as you head into the last part, where I explore how to use design to craft new experiences so the people you care about—your clients, your family members, other residents in your town—can feel more belonging and less othering.

You got this.

Your Moments

In this exercise, I invite you to think through the moments presented here and ask yourself what your version of each moment looks like. Think about a specific context: an organization or team you are part of, the flow of your family's year, the life cycle of your product, or the journey of a new group that is just flickering in your mind's eye. You might have multiple arcs, from someone first joining you on a path to when it all goes up in smoke.

Don't overcomplicate it. Start with what's obvious and then think about what might be in between. Then bring the belonging lens to your map. What are the experiences in real time that could build more belonging, and where is othering a risk? Name those moments so you can see them for what they are.

Explore each moment by asking yourself: *Is this a moment of belonging for us? How does it function? How could we tune it for greater belonging?* After looking at the moments provided, add your own moments too.

If this exercise feels powerful for you, consider doing it with the people you work with. Look at the moments together and come up with your own to focus your efforts.

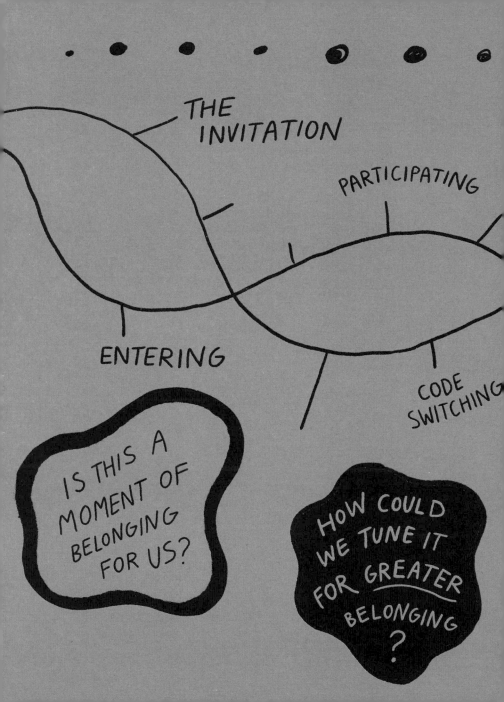

- **Clothing:** It's not as frivolous as it might seem.
- **Food:** Breaking bread together may be the ultimate form of belonging.
- **Schedules and Rhythms:** We live in real time and can better shape it for the world we want to see.

These levers are powerful tools for generating ideas and creating change. They set you up to try new things, engage in different ways, and prototype your ideas with safe-to-fail experiments.

Safe-to-fail experiments are situations where you try things out so people can experience your ideas, while also being mindful to not injure vulnerable groups or rekindle past traumas. They are best done in close collaboration where trust has been built. Safe-to-fail experiments produce signals that we read with our bodies. As you create— whatever you create—think not only with your head but also with your embodied sense of belonging. Ask yourself, *How would that feel? And for whom?* And then don't just imagine how things might turn out; ask questions of others to see how things actually feel. Go beyond your assumptions and try things out. As Claude Steele says in his book *Whistling Vivaldi: How Stereotypes Affect Us and What We Can Do,* "You read the available cues for evidence that you belong." Your work is to craft the building blocks of daily life experiences and ensure that each one builds toward belonging.

Use the levers to reawaken or discover your tinkering self! This is not to say that you should think small; rather, that you should allow your thinking to diverge before you converge. You design for belonging by trying out any and all of the levers you have at your disposal. Each design lever explored on the following pages includes examples and questions that push you to try something new. And trying something new is an invitation to design.

The role of design in belonging is to support outcomes, not mere outputs. What you make is not enough; you must also consider how each lever shapes the moment you are designing for and the resulting feelings that are experienced and by whom. Remember that we have a *sense* of belonging. It's a feeling, and you can't design a feeling. What you *can* design, and what these levers are here to encourage you to explore, are the concrete things you can build in order to set the stage for belonging to emerge. Too often the role of design is to create without taking into consideration what happens next. Whether it's a tangible product, a physical space, a time-based experience, or a social system, design has a responsibility—and by that, I mean we designers have a responsibility—to grapple with what happens in, from, by, and through our designs. We cannot rest on the possibility of our outputs; we must carry on to understand the outcomes of what we create. To this end, use the levers here to truly change the way people experience the world.

Space

Skate park, hotel lobby, mosque. Space is used to construct who is in and who is out. The way a space flows and forms indicates what skills and knowledge are required to enter and to succeed and whether we are allowed to make mistakes. Space can also tell us how to play and what mischief we can make. It offers behavioral clues and cues for how to show up and who is really wanted. You can consciously design a space to be welcoming and inclusive, or you can neglect to—at your peril.

Skate parks are a powerful example of spaces that allow for authentic learning and clear ways into a community. They are obviously not for everyone. But for folks interested in skating and riding BMX bikes, they offer a layered way to practice a craft. Show up and watch or jump in and ride—both are acceptable approaches and part of the learning journey. Admission is usually free, but use of the space is practically dependent on having the gear required: board, bike, helmet, and pads.

Skate parks offer some noticeable ways a space can be crafted for belonging: There are multiple perches for watching and learning, and usually multiple ramps and bowls for different skill levels. As my friend and skate shop owner Patrick told me, the park "is made so you can roll up and see what's happening, then drop in when you are ready."

As much as I love a skate park as a multilayered learning environment, you have to look hard for spaces that offer truly inclusive play, especially for children with disabilities. An excellent model for an explicitly inclusive play space is the Magical Bridge Playground in Palo Alto, California. Designed with a broad mandate to include children with a range of physical and mental abilities, along with their caregivers, its website says its features "are friendly to people with visual impairments, autism, and cognitive disabilities." It also has room for wheelchairs, walkers, and other assistive devices. These features include a slow-moving swing for children who are anxious, a wide ramp with graspable shapes and colors for children who need assistance with climbing, and a harp that is triggered to play when you pass by, to spark joy and curiosity for whoever is able to notice it. There are so many more things to touch, hear, and maneuver than in a traditional playground. As a result, the team that built it has found it to be incredibly popular with a wide range of children and their families, showing that playing together across abilities can be the most fun.

Space considerations can also be subtle. In *Whistling Vivaldi,* social psychologist Claude Steele shows how space can be permeated with cues for belonging (and othering), particularly for underrepresented groups. Through his own story of not being sure he belonged in graduate school as the one Black doctoral student in a program of more than a hundred and through his subsequent research, he establishes the existence and disabling power of *stereotype threat*: the fear that one will live out a negative stereotype based on race, gender, or disability, and how it can cause people to question their belonging in a given context.

The research Steele pioneered and has continued to develop with colleagues shows that, by invoking a negative stereotype of a group, you can undermine the performance of individuals who identify with that group. For example, his research has shown that if you reference poor performance of African Americans or women in computer science before an exam in a computer science class, African Americans or women will do worse than

"If enough cues in a setting can lead members of a group to feel 'identity safe,' it might neutralize the impact of other cues in the setting that could otherwise threaten them."

—CLAUDE STEELE

peers who share their identity but receive a different message. The phenomenon comes from referencing group stigmatization.

To combat this effect, you place cues in your environment to let everyone know they are included. This could mean anything from who is represented in outreach materials to who is included in test questions—whether that representation consists of imagery, stories, or concrete examples of success—you can help people overcome persistent identity threats.

IDEAS FOR SPACE

You don't have to be an architect to use your space to send signals of belonging. Here are some ideas to get you started.

Accommodations Outfitting your space to allow for easy access for people with different kinds of bodies, mobility, and assistive devices is de rigueur. But doing it in ways that feel truly inclusive and caring makes it about belonging. Going beyond the strictly legal, like ramps and railings, is also powerful. For instance, think about how your space works for parents with children, potentially adding a play space, or supporting nursing mothers who need a dedicated, private place to pump that isn't just a broom closet. You might also think about neurodiversity: Do you have spaces for different kinds of thinking—introverts and extroverts—as well as places that allow people to reduce stimulation and meditate?

Resources, Props, and Tools Offer materials that help people to join in. Maybe these are playful items: large balls, foam cubes, or hula hoops. They could be a workshop area with building and craft materials, a spot to choose your own furniture, or a garden shed to get folks outdoors. Or how about a dress-up closet or photo

CLAUDE STEELE

Dr. Claude Steele is a social psychology researcher who
has explored the myriad ways stereotype threat works in
our culture. He is widely published in scholarly journals, and
in his book *Whistling Vivaldi*, he shares his research with
a mainstream audience. His focus is on how understanding
stereotype threat can help us think about how to redesign
our environments for greater belonging.

booth? These can be powerful signals that show you welcome a range of ways of thinking and contributing within your space.

Light Consider which light sources are turned on and off and what dimming or brightening does to the mood. A soft, warm light can create a more intimate setting, whereas a bright light can help people stay energized and focused on a task.

Furniture Moveable furniture gives you the chance to customize for your group size to build in intimacy or accommodate the enthusiasm of a crowd. Notice how a close circle of chairs or couches supports engaging in conversation, whereas large, chunky props can invite building and play.

Outdoor Access and Airflow Let people know that they are part of something bigger than themselves by including an outdoor element in your space. Or enable greater participation by having an airy space with no hard limits on crowd size.

Signage and Media You have incredible opportunities to send belonging cues through the visual stories in your space. Imagine large posters of the clients and community members you serve, or a hallway of monitors telling your founding story and how people can join your work. Keeping Claude Steele's and Carolyn Finney's (page 114) work in mind, consider how visual stories or media could signal belonging for previously marginalized groups and support the belonging narratives you want to see.

Leave a Trace Invite folks to leave some evidence of their work, thinking, or personality behind, such as a photo or tag or symbolic object. Allowing personal touches to accumulate can be a powerful and visible sign of belonging.

~~~~ **Ask Yourself**

- If your space sent signals for how people could belong, what would that look like? Consider your office, the parking lot, the library's community room, and so on.

Roles

Roles are an often overlooked lever of design. There's something about roles that makes them seem inevitable, like somehow we imagine that the roles of concierge or police officer or florist have always been there. But the fact is, they haven't. Roles are designed as part of systems. Consider that social workers, human resources professionals, social media platform monitors, and Walmart greeters are all relatively recent inventions, needed as part of new programs, technologies, and social realities. And because every role is designed, new roles can be designed to foster belonging. They can be long-term positions designed to hold a group's vision or short-term opportunities aimed at specific tasks.

Roles can also be a way to shift group dynamics. When I was teaching a class about design and innovation to some executives, we wondered together how they might help their junior employees build trust and learn that taking some risks is an acceptable thing to do at work. As an experiment, we hired a belly-dance instructor to work with us for an hour. She arrived with a small bag of tricks—beads and scarves—just enough to shift the mood and help everyone recognize that this was no longer business as usual. She then used her life story—the different places she had learned her moves—to invite us to try movements we had never done with our bodies. We worked together in new ways, supporting each other's emerging dances. By the end of our short lesson she had gracefully guided the boss to dance in front of the team—and that made everyone feel safe. Ultimately her role as impromptu instructor shifted the dynamics of the group and allowed us to discuss risk taking at work in a whole new way.

Roles can also be developed to solve a problem. At Playworks, to promote healthy play at school, they designed the role of Recess Coach (adult Americorps volunteers) and Junior Coach (fifth graders!) to support kids in learning new ways to play together, to improve recess, and to build more belonging in elementary school cultures. The new roles support the community on the playground with new games, game instruction, and conflict resolution so that playing together works for everyone.

Roles are designed and can be redesigned. They are invented and can be invented anew. Don't be afraid to tinker with them. Start by evaluating the current roles, the responsibilities at their core, what's been added on, and what remains relevant (or not). Or create a blue-sky version of your organizational chart by asking yourself or your team: *If we could have any roles to support our work, what could they be?* At the end of a year or at another meaningful chapter marker imagine that all roles are sunsetting and ask yourself: *What roles are needed for the new chapter?*

Talking about eliminating roles or creating new ones can be awkward. When discussing the idea of generating new roles, it's important to assure folks that creating roles is a separate conversation from who inhabits the roles. These can be related, but they can also be held as distinct matters.

IDEAS FOR ROLES

Not the head of human resources? That's okay. Play with these archetypes and how they might apply in your context.

Detective Perhaps what's needed to work toward more belonging in your group is some sleuthing. Can you commission someone to investigate how people are really feeling? Maybe there's an incident that has folks on edge, a desire to look at day-to-day workflows, or the need to support a project team that has recently begun to struggle. Once you know more about the group's reality, you can design for change as needed. If the detective has found clues for where greater belonging is needed or has witnessed feelings of being othered, it's time to design. Call together the team to more fully share feelings and findings and generate ideas for change.

Data Head We're often drowning in data, but taking a fresh look can be important. This person can look at the data you have to shed light on what's working, what's not, and for whom. You can humanize the data by pushing yourself to tell new stories with it. If your organization is obsessed with data and seeking to use it in new ways, visualizing multiple interpretations and telling different stories can unlock opportunities to shift dynamics.

Concierge Appoint someone to take the role of attending to the needs of others. As they notice and learn, they will be able to report back on underlying needs that the community might want to address in a more systematic way. For example, the concierge might discover that your elders need support with transportation or that your international participants are looking for ways to stay connected to their culture or need different food options. This discovery can push you to build, using some of the other design levers. Perhaps you can reimagine space, groupings, or food to make your program more inclusive.

Crew Leader for a Day Sometimes seeing a new face at the start of a regular meeting can shake up things that need to get unstuck. Or take this idea further and switch up multiple roles. Make this switch regularly so the team knows this kind of refresh is available when needed. You will learn more about your teammates, and that in turn builds greater belonging.

Ask Yourself

- What roles exist in my group?
- Are they formal, named roles or informal, claimed roles?
- What's a role that you could try out, even briefly, to shift the dynamics of belonging in your team, large or small?

Events

Does the idea of being an event planner excite you or fill you with fear and anxiety? (Either answer is totally cool by me.) Whether big or small, event design is about crafting an experience.

We can be reasonably sure that events are as old as human history. Want to bring two families together? Have a wedding. Want neighbors to have a chance to interact? Create a block party. Want to let parents and caregivers know what is in store for their kiddos? Host a back-to-school night. These are familiar events. To design them for inclusion and belonging raises the bar, inviting in and attending to different dimensions of your community.

The key to successful events is to ensure that belonging is a through line, not just a bullet point. A perfect example of this is the Black Joy Parade in Oakland, California, an event that places belonging as the central premise from which everything builds. During the parade people unabashedly take to the streets to celebrate Black joy. Centering on joy humanizes the Black experience in a way that is often missing in everyday media representations of the Black experience in America.

The event lever is a great one to utilize for the moments of belonging I discussed in the previous part, such as entering, flowing, or even dissenting. What moment in your organization's roster of offerings could use an event? It might be a moment you haven't focused on with much intention or one that needs a refresh, like how people join your business as a new customer or how you grapple with the aftermath of a big decision or cutbacks. Perhaps it's about how people leave your organization—a reimagining of the retirement party as a touchstone for people at all levels. Or an event to celebrate how people are contributing to your community, like when the Oakland As, my local baseball team, celebrate all the kids who have taken part in a summer reading program. It's a big party at the stadium, with fireworks, to honor the work of students, parents, and teachers. Note, however, that not all events are parties. For example, think of the first day of school for a new student or reentry of someone into your group after incarceration.

The power of design comes into bold relief when the people you are designing for are vulnerable. Take someone returning from prison, for instance. Perhaps they have gained important self-knowledge and are ready to chart a new course. They need to be seen and supported for who they are now. Sure, have a party, but also consider other kinds of events that might help them get settled.

No matter which moment you seek to craft, the design should be attended to with care; simply putting it on the calendar is not enough. Prioritize belonging, because if events are not done well, they can be painful experiences of othering, where people feel worse instead of better.

IDEAS FOR EVENTS

Here are some questions and considerations to help you think about event design in terms of belonging.

Why Consider why you want to gather folks and why they would want to join you, your organization, or the group. When you design with purpose, you are pointing yourself in the right direction. When you are explicit about your why, then others can join in based on their whys as well. Examples of whys for events are gathering to raise money, coming together to build and expand a network, engaging in creative problem solving, or reuniting to reminisce about old times. No judgment, just clarity.

Who What kinds of people are you trying to bring together, and what are the dimensions of the group? Where will there be commonalities to build on and differences to bridge? You might be thinking of an event where the people invited come from a purposely narrow group or one that is broadly diverse. Themes can be a powerful way to draw people in across difference. You can consider aspects of identity that will be helpful to make visible, such as work and travel experiences or family backgrounds and configurations. Setting the stage so folks can see themselves belonging through outreach before, during, and after an event can also be supportive.

Where Think about accessibility across as many dimensions as possible in order to support those you want to feel that they belong. This could mean thinking about cognitive as well as physical abilities. Does the space require walking? How would people who are easily overstimulated feel? What about access to public transportation? Location accessibility can also have to do with scale. The Burning Man Festival is held way out in the desert to attract a committed crowd, seeking to be off the beaten track to build an event that is also an experiment in communal living.

When Thinking about who will attend will help you think about how time plays a role. Consider work schedules, family commitments, religious practices. Is there a specific date or time that would lend meaning to the event?

What With the previous questions answered, the *what* can come into view. The only limit here is your imagination. Host a joyous brainstorm; go broad before you narrow down to one approach. To fuel your brainstorm, try working a metaphor (see page 26). Some examples: Our event will feel like a private tour with a forest ranger so that people know they are in good hands and can explore with knowledge at their beck and call. Our volunteer recognition party will feel like a trip to a country fair where everyone is comfortable in their casual clothes and there are so many kinds of pie you can't stop grinning so that people can relax and have fun. Our staff retreat will feel like we're falling down the rabbit hole in *Alice in Wonderland* so that even the most introverted team members will feel comfortable sharing their dreams for the future.

Ask Yourself

- What is a meaningful moment in your community, organization, or family that could use an event?

- What will it take for us to focus it on belonging?

- How will my events ensure that vulnerable people or groups are not othered?

Rituals

As a subset of events, rituals offer a chance to focus on personal, interpersonal, or communal meaning-making, and you can consciously design them to any scale to reduce othering and promote belonging. Rituals help us notice and feel the meaning of our lives. Coming-of-age ceremonies, like bar and bat mitzvahs or quinceañeras, and some kinds of induction ceremonies are specifically designed for joining a community and taking up its practices. Rituals can also be so deeply meaningful when they happen that you feel their absence too. Think of the people who had to put off funerals during COVID-19 shutdowns, and how hard it might have been to process grief without the ritual of a memorial service to mark the passing of a loved one.

To be successful, rituals should have a beginning, a middle, and an end. In fact, neuroscience research has shown that each of these parts plays an important role. The beginning, which could be an act such as bowing or other gestures as you enter a sacred space, tells your brain that you can release yourself from your normal concerns; you're entering a special time and place. The middle, or what is called the *enactment*, puts you in a receptive mode, where you're open to new wisdom. And finally, the end, which could perhaps be a meal or a blessing, is a celebration of what you have learned or experienced. In simple terms, within a ritual you need to get grounded and join in, spend some time chewing on what really matters, and conclude with a new understanding that you take with you.

Although we seem to accept centuries-old rituals like dissertation defenses or graduation processionals without too much question, it is much rarer to design our own. It's something we're certainly capable of doing, however: Think about fresh takes on commitment ceremonies and do-it-yourself, coming-of-age rituals. Purpose matters for ritual design. Your ritual might be explicitly about building belonging or, more often, about something else you and your community need to accomplish. Once you've identified the need, you have the opportunity to consciously attend to belonging as part of it. Ask yourself: *Are we opening the year or closing a project? Is it for me as an individual or for the whole group? Are we trying to create something that happens regularly or that marks a transition?*

While working with a K–8 school in Oakland called Urban Montessori, I helped the team create a back-to-school ritual in which families came together to share their skills. We opened with a community coffee circle. The main enactment was a design thinking process where each parent designed something for another parent: a calendar noting ways to participate at school, a custom T-shirt featuring the school's logo and the family's name, a totem to remind the parent that they had things to share with the community. Everyone had something created for them, as the group wanted to explicitly recognize that everyone, regardless of their privilege, had something to teach the group and could each make something for another. We closed by sharing what we had made and offering gratitude for our time together. By building in the purpose of getting to know and support each other, this effort became an important community ritual.

Betty Ray, formerly an online community builder and now founder of the Center for Ritual Design, helps individuals and groups with rituals. According to Betty, one way to create a recurring ritual is to build it on something that is already happening. It could be your weekly trip to the grocery store or your evening dog walk or, in the context of work, a weekly meeting or quarterly report. For instance, during the recent global pandemic Betty worked with someone who was seeking to create a new morning ritual. He found that he was spending an hour doom scrolling every morning, and it was a terrible way to start the day. To shift it, they reconsidered his morning coffee. The beverage could stay, but he replaced the doom scrolling with taking his coffee into the garden to enjoy with his partner, followed by a morning walk together. Betty said, "The shift was huge. Consciously designing for that moment instead of picking up the phone by default made all the difference."

As with each design lever, the power to create change for greater belonging comes from consciously choosing to attend to what's not working and then explicitly crafting something different to change the dynamics. As you line up your needs, ideas for rituals may naturally come into form. Remember the goal for the rituals you design is a stronger sense of belonging.

IDEAS FOR RITUALS

Here are some starting points for ritual design.

Identify the Need Consider where and how a ritual might aid your group. Do you need inspiration to start something new or motivation to continue an ongoing project? Do you want to celebrate or recognize a completed task or a job well done? Is there a way to incorporate a ritual into a recurring event or meeting? You might use the check-in question for your crew to learn more about each other. You could do shout-outs at the top of a meeting to support the need for acknowledgment and gratitude.

Source Inspiration Mine the rituals you know—from childhood, school, your last job—to get ideas, then design or redesign them for new circumstances. It could be spirit week, decorating for the change of seasons, or assigning secret partners for gift giving. Also explore symbols or artifacts that might have meaning for your group. Maybe there are artifacts from people's ancestral homes or an altar. When drawing from other cultures, be sure to seek advice so you don't appropriate concepts, gestures, or forms without understanding and consideration. You can also bring in the senses—aroma, color, and texture can all contribute to the tone of what you create.

Open Begin your ritual with a form of release or inspiration. It could be a circle where each person sees and acknowledges the other with a check-in or a grounding meditation. Tapping into the senses can be another form of opening: Read poetry, light a candle, play music.

Act Go somewhere, do something, say something, make something. This is the heart of the ritual. In a vision quest, this is your time alone on the mountain. Closer to home, this might be an interaction among the team members, like a service project or building something collaboratively. It might be sharing gifts, literally or figuratively. It could also be a structured conversation designed to generate insight or understanding.

Close Celebrate the connections made, learning gained, or milestone achieved. The closing could be a dance party or more serious expressions of gratitude. This is the opportunity to incorporate the specialness of your ritual into daily life. It is your journey forward into other parts of your life or your community's work. A closing circle, where you literally stand in a circle, might include sharing learnings or appreciations, either at length or with just a word. Sometimes inviting each person into the circle to be acknowledged and celebrated is powerful. The flavor can match your group; it could be cacophonous applause or total silence.

Ask Yourself

- What's a need in my community?
- How might the structure of a new ritual help to address it?
- What rituals are already present, and how might they be radically redesigned or subtly tuned to be more inclusive?

Grouping

Designing for how people come together as groups can be a powerful part of your belonging toolkit. We all have multiple contexts in our lives, and we feel belonging in more than one group. It's likely that we also feel differently in different group settings.

Sociology is an entire field dedicated to group formation and exploring the myriad ways groups come together. In a business context, you might have heard of teams going through the stages of "norming, storming, forming, performing," processes that groups are often seen experiencing as they get to know each other, understand each other's skills and strengths, and begin to work together effectively. For the purpose of belonging, we can design groups intentionally to cut across boundaries and help people bond across differences. You can design groups that support one aspect of a person's identity over another, or you can design groups that invite people to show up and share as many aspects of themselves as they can.

In a heterogeneous group it is often important to bring forward identities that may be inadvertently hidden. For example, I have been part of an extremely diverse university-based group drawn from all different disciplines and with a mixture of ages and racial identities. When we came together, we each declared who we were standing for in the group as a way to honor our various identities. Folks literally said, "I stand for first-generation college students." "I stand for working parents with young children." "I stand on the shoulders of my enslaved ancestors." And we went round and round the circle until we had exhausted the "stand fors" we wanted to share. By exposing the hidden aspects of our identities and histories, we opened ourselves up to building different connections than we had at first known were available.

A specific example of groups that can support feelings of belonging is the structure known as racial affinity groups. These communities are designed for exploring identity and the historical legacy of racial discrimination and White supremacy in the United States. Used extensively in the work of racial justice, these groups ask people to self-identify their racial identity and join the corresponding group.

The National Equity Project and other anti-racist organizations teach the practices of affinity groups during workshops designed to support cross-racial problem solving and the dismantling of systems of oppression. There is power in group identity to ground learning and prepare for work across difference to reduce othering. Explorations can be wide-ranging, and they often help participants see how aspects of identity show up in collaborative work, what the consequences are, and how to change them.

For Black and Brown people, affinity groups can offer spaces of healing and support, building resilience for other contexts. For White people, affinity groups can be used to learn how to be anti-racist while not burdening people of color with caretaking for their learning or emotions. When used in this way, the structure recognizes that the work White people have to do to dismantle White supremacy culture is theirs to do, and that the Black participants are not responsible for supporting White people in their unlearning. As awkward and retrograde as it can feel to gather exclusively as White people, the existence of these groups themselves establishes a sense of belonging for all involved because they show a commitment to taking responsibility for learning.

It may seem surprising or counterintuitive to separate as a way to foster inclusion, but it allows groups to process their feelings and potential past traumas. The benefit of this kind of grouping is the focus on healing and learning in the group with which you identify, often as a way to prepare for intergroup dialogue.

Showing solidarity as part of an affinity group can also be powerful. In the wake of the police killing of George Floyd in the summer of 2020, among the many protest images was a video of a group of Mennonites protesting in Minneapolis alongside other marchers. It was an example of one subgroup showing up in support of another. The video went viral, likely because of its poignant reminder of the relative rarity—or at least lack of visibility—of images of cross-group solidarity. In addition to race, affinity group structures can be established around other aspects of identity, including gender, class, physical abilities, or job role.

As a lever of design, groups aren't limited to affinity groups. In design classes at the d.school, we often explicitly construct groups to mix up backgrounds. Research on team dynamics has shown that in order to generate breakthrough ideas, you can be well served by having groups with different disciplinary backgrounds. There are likely infinite ways to arrange your groups, such as support groups or group therapy, but to build belonging, you want to be explicit about what you hope to achieve as you design your group structures.

Groups might be formed related to any of the moments of belonging. For instance, think about groups that are part of the invitation to or entering of a program or organization. You might be welcomed into a class or cohort, but maybe just being new isn't enough of a connection, so you call upon another aspect of identity to bond with as part of joining a new context. Family camps have grown in popularity because they support parents and children in getting to know camping in the outdoors with other families, bringing people together not because they are expert but because they want to find a place and to be a part of something (the outdoors) as an expression of another aspect of their identity (family). Groups are often formed to express dissent. Think of any recent protest movement—Black Lives Matter or the Women's March or Extinction Rebellion—people came together to express discontent and to promote hope for a different future. The purpose of these types of groupings is to belong to something bigger than yourself. Conjuring these massive movements is a reminder that you can design for group participation at any scale to support purposeful belonging.

IDEAS FOR GROUPING

Groups can, of course, take innumerable shapes and pathways. Your work when pulling this lever is to be intentional. Here are some things to think about.

Purpose This is where your leadership shows. Name the purpose of the group that will come together. Who are you bringing together, and why?

People Given that we are talking about belonging, do you seek to bring folks together to work across difference, or is it about affinity groups? Offering parameters and the reasoning behind them is helpful to everyone.

Shape and Size Small and intimate, or large and raucous. Are you open to an ebb and flow of participants? If the group starts out one way and needs to grow or shrink, will that feel okay?

Duration You may form your group for a one-time event—a breakout at a workshop, for example. But if the grouping is meant to endure, think about how people come and go and how relationships and knowledge are carried forward. What else will be required to keep it going, if that is desired?

Support Structures In addition to group meeting agendas, think about group structures. How will people meet together? Are there ground rules? Group agreements can help people share the air, establish understanding around confidentiality, or build comfort with potential for closure or anticipating lack of closure. Seek or create structures such as constructivist listening dyads, in which a pair takes turns speaking on a topic with a focus on the benefit the speaker receives from being heard. Or to make large group conversation more intimate and productive, the World Cafe structure utilizes small group tables where one person at each hosts a topic for discussion and people can move from table to table while contributing to work on different topics. As with most of our design levers, trying things out and modifying to ensure meaningful inclusion is the way to go.

Ask Yourself

- What groups am I part of? Do any of them need to be redesigned to promote greater belonging?

- Are there any aspects of my identity that are hidden in a group that I would like to bring forward?

- Where in my life and work would an affinity group help me learn about myself or get support needed for my growth and development? What about for others I would like to support?

Communications

In many contexts, communications is the lever of design that's easiest to pick up, and it is often the one used with most abandon. We are always sending explicit and implicit messages about who belongs and who doesn't, who can thrive and who might not get the support they need. So if you craft a lot of communications—memos, emails, signage—you've gotta work hard and get it right. Representation matters. You may have heard that phrase, but it is worth repeating.

Whether you are thinking about your coworkers, your clients, or your program participants, the people you engage deserve authentic representations of who and how your program or organization supports people. Craft your communications so that they help a wide range of people to see themselves invited in, participating fully, achieving flow, and moving through all the moments of belonging that matter.

Don't forget that what you leave out sends a message too. Carolyn Finney, a geographer, scholar, and author of *Black Faces, White Spaces: Reimagining the Relationship of African Americans to the Outdoors,* looks closely at the national parks and mainstream environmental organizations to reveal how few Black people are shown in their communications. Finney, like bell hooks (page 23), had a childhood connected to the outdoors, living on a woodsy estate where her parents were caretakers. She had a strong personal sense of belonging in nature, and she viscerally experienced the lack of Black representation in nature, in media generally, and in publications related to the environmental movement.

These omissions have power, and they create vicious cycles. If we don't see someone represented somewhere, we don't build their belonging into the rest of our programming. And these omissions have real consequences. For instance, while he was birdwatching in New York's Central Park, Christian Cooper, a Black man, was called in to the authorities by an aggressive White woman when he asked her to leash her dog. He posed no threat to her and was simply asking her to

CAROLYN FINNEY

Dr. Carolyn Finney is a writer, performer, and cultural geographer. Her book *Black Faces, White Spaces: Reimagining the Relationship of African Americans to the Great Outdoors* explores the cultural history of racializing the outdoors. Her analysis shows us how we might use representation and other inclusion practices to create change.

obey the posted rule, but she reported him, counting on the policing system to interpret a Black man in nature as a threat. This story is a bald example of how our imagination of who belongs where is shaped by the accumulation of representations.

A great example of a communications campaign that explicitly responded to a lack of representation is #ilooklikeanengineer. The campaign is still being used to spotlight women of color who are engineers in a field dominated by White men. Hashtags abound and can be a playful and powerful way to bridge ideas. Choose your tonic or design your own.

"Stories become the vehicles we use to define ourselves and the places we inhabit and utilize. So, whose stories are being told? Whose pictures do we see?"

—CAROLYN FINNEY

Beyond (e)mail and digital campaigns, how we talk about what our group or community represents is at the core of communication. With this in mind, it's important to understand that all communications—the subtle and the explicit—contribute strongly to the ways we form our own narratives about what is happening and whether or not we belong. They shape our self-talk, and our self-talk informs what we believe is possible.

If you come from a less-resourced background, it can be particularly hard to be the first person from your family, neighborhood, or country to join an institution. At the University of Texas, psychology scholar David Yeager and

> "Ultimately a person has within themselves some kind of capital, some kind of asset, like knowledge or confidence. And if we can help bring that out, they then carry that asset with them to the next difficulty in life."
>
> —DAVID YEAGER

his colleagues showed that having even relatively short interventions, including videos and outreach from older students, can alleviate the fear of not belonging for first-generation college students.

Psychologically speaking, these students can interpret doing poorly on an exam as either a sign that *I need to study more* or a sign that *I don't belong.* What Yeager's team did was simple. They asked current students from similar backgrounds to tell their stories in short videos—including and normalizing some of the ups and downs of moving away from home and getting used to college life. For example, the students talk about getting a poor grade on a test and then studying harder for the next one. The researchers found that sharing these short videos with new students helped them adjust. Instead of feeling like they did not belong when they hit a common bump in any new student's college experience, they persevered. The videos help students focus on actions that help them become better students, such as going to a study group or reaching out to a professor, instead of feeling they don't belong. These interventions and others like them contributed to the university dramatically raising the four-year graduation rate for first-generation students.

DAVID YEAGER

Dr. David Yeager is a professor at the University of Texas, Austin. His work on growth mindset intersects with our understanding of belonging. You can find his work in scholarly journals and through the Mindset Scholars Network as well in *The Years That Matter Most: How College Makes or Breaks Us* by Paul Tough.

For me, two things really jump out from this work. First, the fear of not belonging is really powerful, and you need to be on the lookout for it. Investigate where it is showing up in your programs, perhaps even in your extended family. Second, it doesn't take a huge effort to help people dive into what is in front of them instead of look for the exit. This research shows that stories are powerful design tools; they shape our environments and our thinking.

IDEAS FOR COMMUNICATIONS

Here are some key features for using communications to support belonging.

Clear Audience Know who you are speaking to and why. Is this a new audience for you or your organization? Think about how the people to whom you are reaching out self-identify, and respect the language that is important to those individuals or groups.

Focused Message In all communications, clarity of purpose matters. If you are using communications to build bridges from othering to belonging, know the history you are part of, then point to a potential shared future. For example, in recent voter registration drives run by Fair Fight in Georgia, the organization clearly referenced the history of Black voter disenfranchisement as part of the get-out-the-vote message.

Opportunities to Engage Ensure that someone who thinks they might belong knows how to enter, join, and participate. Build their confidence so they can move from *Is it for me?* to *They want me!* To soothe fears that the recipient of your communications might not belong, offer concrete examples and cues by visualizing the range of people you are hoping to engage. Acknowledge complexities and open two-way channels for communication—sharing where you are in a growth process both humanizes the work you are doing and invites people to be a part of something. Recall that the ability to make demands is a measure of belonging—set yourself up to welcome feedback, critique, and new ideas.

Ask Yourself

- What communication mechanism (email, phone, in person) do I use as a default? How could I alter the medium (from email to in person, for example)? Could I offer more powerful feelings of belonging through the message—that is, how I'm saying what I'm saying?

- What stories and representations support my belonging in my work and home?

- What uncertainties are faced by the people I work with? Is there a new story that would support greater belonging?

Picture Grid Conversation

We know the adage, "A picture is worth a thousand words," yet so often we forget it. As you launch into the world of shaping or reshaping belonging in your context, pictures can be a grounding way to have a desired conversation. Offer images to prompt a conversation, and use them to talk about what is working and what is not.

Select a set of images with different emotional qualities— a bouncy puppy, a sad-seeming elder, a serene mountain lake, a screaming baby in a stroller. Print them out or put them into a slide deck so you can show them to somebody else. Then have a conversation. Ask, "Which image feels like the state of belonging in our family, town, or organization? Why? What makes you say that?"

Because you started with an almost random set of images, you'll likely hear some really interesting things about what is and is not working in the context—things you might not have discovered if you asked the question without an image. Extend the conversation by reflecting back what you heard and inquiring whether they have ideas for growth or changes. Ask them to share an image of their own that represents their sense of belonging and follow up to learn why.

Clothing

Clothing as a design lever might seem somewhat trivial, but it can be both a profound symbol and a powerful tool in the work of belonging. Take, for example, how former supreme court justice Ruth Bader Ginsburg added a special collar to her judge's robe. As she became famous (aka the Notorious RBG), versions of her collar became a form of wearable solidarity. Women around the world added collars literally to their physical clothes and digitally to their photographs to band together in support of women's rights.

World history also offers myriad—and sometimes shocking—examples of clothing used to mark groups and to explicitly other some people. I'm thinking of the Nazi Brownshirts and the stars of David that Jewish people were forced to wear during World War II. The swastika created a bond among Hitler's recruits; others were forced to salute them. The star was forced on Jewish people to separate and victimize them. The symbols and the clothing on which they were displayed worked in concert to privilege one group over another.

Just as clothing can separate us, it can also be a way to bring people together. Clothing and gear can also be shorthand for affinity groups to understand who shares their norms and, presumably, their values. Schools, for instance, prohibit certain clothing items from being worn in order to cut down on gang activity. These actions attack a surface representation in hopes of uprooting a deeper sense of belonging that is perceived as negative.

You really can't talk about clothes and belonging without talking about the gear that sports fans don. Indeed, all professional sports teams have a ton of gear, but the Green Bay Packers get special points for their cheesehead. To state the obvious, while every team in the NFL offers hats (yes, I checked), only one team has a cheesehead. I don't know if it causes the fans to feel an even greater sense of belonging, but it may not be a coincidence that the most unique headgear in the NFL is sported by the fans of the only team owned by a public nonprofit. Those cheeseheads own the team.

I hadn't thought about sports gear much until a colleague, a successful leader in the philanthropy field, mentioned how she suits up to go to soccer games. She's a Black woman from the American South and did not grow up with soccer, but she married an Englishman. ('Nough said?) The clothes are her way in. As she told me, "It's a uniform. I put it on and I am a part of it. It doesn't matter that I didn't grow up with the sport. Now I'm in. All in." She didn't have to pass an entrance exam on the finer points of offsides calls in order to be part of the scene. The jersey (and her husband, to be sure) made her part of the scene. Donning the garb gave her easier entry into the club and made it "kinda fun."

Teams, concerts, schools, and camps: Any organization with an event, ritual, or rhythm likely has some gear. Notice which ones make you want to join in and belong. Consider dress codes and uniforms. While school uniforms can be constraining to some, they have been shown to help kids work together because they remove some of the markers of wealth and privilege, creating less distraction and more cohesiveness among the students. And, of course, gangs and even more mundane friend groups use clothes to show their membership and their allegiances.

It feels materialistic to focus on clothes as a lever of design, and yet, it is one. Clothing is also included here to remind you that design is around us constantly. If belonging remains consciously in focus as you use the available levers, you can turn something as simple as a T-shirt into a decent tool.

IDEAS FOR CLOTHING

Here are some starting points for making clothes part of your approach.

Get the Tone Right If you're gonna do a team T-shirt, a hat, or even a fanny pack, make it fun. Give it some flavor so folks get the feeling of your team or organization every time they put on the gear.

Volition Making something mandatory doesn't work super well if you want to generate joy for the wearers of your stuff. You usually want to go for willing participation in the gear category so that folks can opt in.

Diversity Within a Look To keep belonging front and center, allowing room for customization is key. No one wants a straitjacket. Make your gear as broadly appealing as your fan base, then sit back and watch how people modify it.

Ask Yourself

- How do you use clothing in your program or community? And if you don't already, how could you?
- How could you imagine using gear to help people feel like part of your organization?
- Which feeling related to belonging—playfulness, solidarity, tenacity—could you support in new ways?

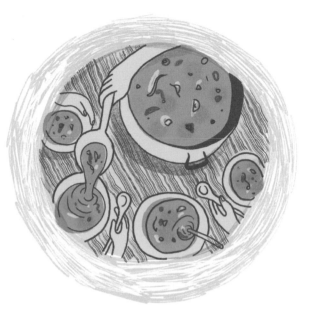

Food

When I ask people to share a time or place where they felt belonging, food comes up as part of the story a huge percentage of the time. It was when their mother-in-law cooked for them for the first time, the end-of-year gathering at work where everyone contributed something, or that potluck picnic back in their hometown.

Breaking bread together is a communal act that often equates with belonging. It is quite literally a signal that you belong, because you are worth nourishing. For example, the Big Table in Columbus, Ohio, is a city-wide dinner with more than ten thousand participants. You can self-organize a table or join an open one. Someone in the community hosts the food, which could be a restaurant donation, a purchase, a home-cooked meal, or a potluck. The event sets the table for belonging through conversation over a meal; the opportunity to connect is what matters.

Another example of this belonging-through-nourishing comes from Angela McKee-Brown, a food thinker as well as a design thinker whom I met while she was a fellow at the d.school. She knows that healthy food matters to sustain our bodies, and healthy food systems have the potential to sustain our communities. When she led school food design services at the San Francisco Unified School District, she worked with students to redesign their lunchrooms. As she got to know the kids in her design research, she saw how much othering happens around food. The "ewws" and the "gross, what's that?" occasionally led young people to throw away their lunches. And for students receiving free and reduced-price lunches, for some the stigma associated with those meals would sometimes lead them to not eat at all. For a student who is food insecure at home and then not eating at school because they feel othered simply by picking up their food, it's a recipe for ongoing hunger and reduced learning. McKee-Brown used these observations and insights to redesign the flow and experience of lunch, in addition to changing the menu to be more culturally responsive and enticing so students were motivated to eat.

Now at the Edible Schoolyard, McKee-Brown brings together her deep knowledge of food with her desire to use design to support communities. In Stockton, California, where many of the residents have lost touch with their agricultural roots despite living less than an hour's drive from one of the most productive farming areas in the world, she is building a new program of school gardens and community meals. The Edible Schoolyard advocates for the connection between the food we eat and where it comes from. Their school-based farms support meals in the schools where they reside. The farm-to-table meals that McKee-Brown organizes are about belonging to each other and to the land that produces so much bounty.

An event organized around food doesn't have to be complicated or fussy. Sometimes the food is just an excuse to bring people together or a chance to have a conversation you need to have. Structure a food gathering to make it explicit, or let it be organic, as meals have likely been for millennia. Given the very primal nature of food, paying attention to how and when it is a part of your community opens it up as a lever for designing for belonging.

IDEAS FOR FOOD

When considering how to use food to promote belonging in your group, meals are a good place to start.

Breakfast Bring people together to start their day. Use the time to set intentions about what's ahead. Use a fun check-in question to let people get to know each other. (If you could eat only one food what would you choose? If you were an animal, what would you be and why? What was your first concert?) Recognize that different people start their days with different energies, so the option to pass might be important.

Lunch Mix up the group's daily habit. Heading outside to get some air or to check out the view shifts the energy. Reach out to someone you don't know well and invite them to lunch at your favorite spot. Make it a potluck where everyone brings a favorite childhood dish or something special from their cultural heritage. These can all be quick wins on the road to belonging.

Dinner The dinner party is a classic gathering. Give it new life with careful attention to who is invited and how they are welcomed. Bring in the notion of a Jeffersonian dinner, where everyone speaks to one question or topic with no side conversations or follow-up questions.

Dessert Use it to celebrate and honor the sweetness of life and milestones. Invite people to share stories about favorite sweets from other times in their life. Pair it with music, generating a playlist of people's favorite songs.

Midnight Snack Honor the night shift with a surprise. Whose work is often unseen? Let them feel the love of community. Or maybe it's a moment for new groupings, depending on who shows up. What might the night owls want to leave behind for others to find in the morning?

And Don't Forget the Recipe Box Collecting and sharing recipes from your campers, workshop participants, or extended family can be a great way to make concrete the kind of belonging we find in food. It has been done before, but is always unique based on who's in your group. You can add a theme that's super narrow, like tacos or pasta dishes or recipes handed down, or make it broad and ask everyone for a favorite dish they want to share. It's even richer if you get people's stories about the recipes and where they came from.

Ask Yourself

- What foods have meaning for you? Which ones do you want to share with your community?
- What could you cook up to bring people together?

Schedules and Rhythms

Schedules can be the beating heart of an organization, but only if they are designed to support people and their needs. When rhythms get established, they can hold many of the moments of belonging. Crafting shared rhythms can be a wonderful way to establish community and bring people in. Using time as a creative lever with which to design can unlock all kinds of cultural norms and create new places for people to show up authentically.

Unfortunately, in lots of places—schools and community-based organizations, government, and companies—the daily, weekly, and yearly rhythms are based on legacy needs, reflecting who was meant to belong in some other time.

School calendars are based on agrarian community models from a time when many children were needed as field hands during the summer. Efforts at year-round school have been tried—and indeed they show better learning outcomes for kids—but still rare is the community where year-round school has become the norm.

Old rhythms can be entrenched, expected, and perhaps beloved. (What child doesn't want a summer vacation?) It's difficult to shift. To use time to shape belonging, you have to really show people what a shift will create. Sometimes that's easier said than done, but you can do it with pop-ups or experiential prototypes. For example, when redesigning the daily schedule that wasn't working at a new elementary school, we took one afternoon and ran a version of the new schedule. We compressed the times a bit, but we made sure we experienced all the transitions—and, wow, was that enlightening! We saw right away that our brilliant idea had kids moving around way more than they could handle while also staying grounded in the relationships we want to support them in. You don't have to build Rome in a day. Start small and build on the ideas that generate the kinds of connections you are hoping to support.

Make schedules as a way to help set rhythms—for connecting, sharing, working, learning—that support belonging. Perhaps there's a weekly meal where people share stories, a monthly dance party, a quarterly opportunity to bring your child to work, or new check-in meetings where people can openly raise concerns.

Once you have milestones, you have opportunities for belonging. Use these newly created moments on the calendar to invite newcomers or for community celebrations. They can even be a place where dissent is heard from across the community.

I'm also a fan of using schedules to disrupt. When launching a new initiative at the d.school, I frequently found it fruitful to have what I call a "prototyping season" that lasted two weeks or more. The goal was to disrupt regular rhythms and get as many people as possible from different points of view to build and test prototypes together around a shared theme. Like a specially organized offsite meeting, this take on a season can be powerful for shifting the way a group spends its days. In addition to getting cool projects rolling, prototyping season always demonstrated how new people could work together when given the chance to escape their daily tasks. This is a real boon for new teams and relationships to emerge and create belonging.

The tech world has seen wide adoption of the daily stand-up meeting. It's literally a meeting where everyone stands, which keeps it brief and focused. Everyone on the team shares a short update: what they did yesterday, what they're working on today, and any help needed. This makes it possible to hear from everyone daily, and this kind of team visibility can be a plus for belonging.

I also love the power of the check-in question: one question used at the beginning of a meeting to bring folks together.

It helps to set the level of participation, ensuring that everyone's voice is heard. The question can be deep or frivolous. What task is on top for you right now? On whose shoulders are you standing today? If you could take a trip anywhere in the world, where would you go? Use this question to humanize any collective moment, and ask the same question of everyone assembled. Individuals can answer in any way that is comfortable for them. Added to different types of meetings, the check-in question becomes a rhythm and a ritual in and of itself.

IDEAS FOR SCHEDULES AND RHYTHMS

Use the natural rhythms within your organization to play with your group's daily, monthly, and seasonal calendar.

Calendar Get one and make it public. Calendars that the whole group uses are the best. Think about how everyone sees it, and get excited about the rhythms it represents or could inspire. For example, with a monthly adventure day on the calendar you have this great opening for people to show up to design and lead something for the group. Of course, the calendars could be digital, but if you are in a shared physical space, consider what my pals at the design thinking studio Stoked Project created—a giant monthly wall calendar—to invite people to envision the future together.

Seasons The natural world gives us great clues for rhythms to follow. If we tune to the emergent energy of spring or the withdrawing energy of winter, we can find connections that ground our work in something bigger than ourselves. Or, like the prototyping season described earlier, create your own seasons that are synchronized with the needs of your crew and those you seek to help.

Make It Personal Sometimes when we think about schedules, our mind can wander to a dry and cranky place, full of obligations or to-dos. Instead, consider the joy of mixing people up in new ways, of creating enough space in the calendar for people to find new ways of working together and new relationships. Keep humans at the center of the rhythms of time and calendar to build belonging. This can be as simple as offering an employee the chance to name a schedule need they have or creating times for personal sharing.

Sunsetting Avoid the tyranny of a packed schedule by creating regular opportunities to eliminate the rhythms that aren't working or are no longer needed. This could be a monthly calendar review. A wise rule is to not add to the calendar unless you have taken something off. It's hard to hold the line, but it's a great goal.

Ask Yourself

- Who does the current schedule prioritize?
- Is there a way to make our schedule truly reflect our community and its needs?
- How can we set rhythms that build in greater belonging?

Meeting Maker

In much of the working world, meetings are the unit of gathering. You step out of your cubicle and into another space to sit and meet. Or you log in to the virtual world and just click on a video conferencing application. Because meetings can take on a kind of "it's always been this way" quality, they are a great place to start changing your culture. In some places, just saying that you are going to design a meeting can be a radical act.

Pick a meeting: Best, worst, or somewhere in between. Then look across the design levers and choose one to pull. Here are some suggestions for how to tune your meeting for belonging.

- **Space:** Consciously pick the space you will use—physical or virtual. Make it fit. You want the space to be right for your group's session, not a generic one, and not last week's, either.

- **Role:** Get clear ahead of time about who is coming and what roles people will play. And focus on roles needed for belonging. Who will welcome new people? Who will honor the need for dissent? Who will support needs for accommodations of different kinds?

- **Event:** Think about your meeting as an event, and craft the experience. Is there music? Lighting? Special guests? Food?

- **Ritual:** Open and close the meeting explicitly. Try a check-in question to start and a one-word checkout to close.

More Levers

Are there more design levers? Indeed. Opportunity for design abounds.

The nine explored here are a good start. They are intended to illuminate this approach to making change by designing and/or redesigning the structures that shape your context. You get to think (and make!) beyond what currently exists.

Some other levers to explore could be:

Avatars: The dimensions on which you can customize them are ripe for greater attention.

Curriculum: Explore concrete ways to teach and learn.

Graphics: The visual world cues so much of our understanding.

Media: We know how much representation matters for belonging.

Online Experiences: Whether it is shopping, gaming, or working, as people spend more and more time online, how you belong increases in importance.

Organizations: This could be building new ones or tuning how an existing organization works.

Policy and Law: We don't always have access to these levers, but we should not ignore them when we seek to understand how to change the systems in which we live and operate.

Practices: Consider all the ways we show up and interact with one another.

Programs: These can go beyond showing up to an event to being part of something over time.

Social Media: Whether on existing or future platforms, intentional design for their use is important.

Social Structures: Beyond organization, how else do people come together?

Keep the list going and design with your own levers. The questions to ask yourself are: *What can I design? And if I design it, will it support others to belong?* In fact, if you can design it, you can design it to promote belonging and eliminate othering.

Design an Action to Build Belonging

Here's a simple framework to help you put your thoughts into action. Remember *Mad Libs*? Well, they're back. Use this frame to generate design actions. The simple format combines *who* plus a *moment of belonging* plus a *design lever*.

How might we support more belonging for

_____
(person/people you are thinking about)

by focusing on _____
(a moment that might matter to them)

using _____ ?
(a design lever that is interesting to you/them)

Take five minutes to fill in the blanks. Repeat the exercise as many times as possible in the time allotted. The completed Mad Libs are now your brainstorm prompts. On your own or with a group, creatively answer the question of how you might support the named person or people in a meaningful moment using different levers. Once you have generated a wide range of ideas, focus in on the idea with the greatest appeal and enact it in the scrappiest, most safe-to-fail version you can try right away. Rinse and repeat.

As with all actions intended to bring about greater belonging, pay careful attention to what actually happens when you enact your idea. What did you notice about people's experiences? Did you support more belonging? If yes, how? If no, what can you change for next time?

Always Choose Belonging

The key to designing for belonging is to make a habit of it. Small actions lead to deeper understanding and the opportunity to see things anew. As you take up the opportunities in your life to design for belonging, you try and then you reflect. A positive impact can spur you on; a negative one is important data you can use to try again.

To encourage full participation, you need to support people's identities, abilities, and values and plan to be responsive to emergent needs. That's a tall order, to be sure, yet it is a big part of what we are endeavoring to do when we design for belonging.

Paying attention matters. How else will you notice who feels belonging and who doesn't, or whether these feelings are predictable, and if so, how? Whether design is your profession or just the way you move in the world, we all constantly bring about change in ways large and small. Focus on how to pay attention to the outcomes of your designs as they emerge, and choose to craft change in a way that promotes belonging, reduces othering, and builds bridges in a complex world. It matters for you up close and personal and in the work you do for the greater good.

The times might feel turbulent or not. Racism or xenophobia may be on the news. A police shooting or an exposé of discrimination or exploitation may be in the headlines. Or maybe it is a slow news day. Regardless, belonging matters.

It matters every day.

Tune yourself to see the system at play. Embolden yourself to try new things to create change. This is not change for change's sake. It is change designed to reduce othering. This is a sliver and a slice of what belonging feels like and how we can design for more people, more often, in more places. It matters because without belonging we can't function in our small groups, let alone confront the big, systemic challenges.

Don't let the hardest challenges paralyze you. Take action, and choose to design for belonging now.

Honor a Place of Belonging

In community workshops, artist Christine Wong Yap (page 20) creates space for people to reflect on the places where they feel belonging. She asks each person to articulate what belonging is for them, and then, if they choose, to create a declaration. She then turns the declarations into beautifully calligraphed posters and delivers them to the places where the belonging occurred— a community center, for sure, but also the apartment where someone's art practice emerged. When it's possible, the person and the organization turn the presentation into an event, offering gratitude and celebrating belonging. This exercise is inspired by Yap's work.

Create a "place of belonging" certificate to give to a space or organization where you feel a deep sense of belonging. In your declaration, you might share what makes the place special, such as a specific memory, or simply extend an expression of gratitude for being a place of belonging for you or your tribe. You could make a beautiful piece of art or just a simple printout, framed or not. If a certificate doesn't feel appropriate, consider a letter or phone call; sharing gratitude is good for all and builds belonging in and of itself.

Acceptance, self-worth, and confidence might all emerge when you think about a place where you feel you belong. Yap encourages us to engage with our feelings and to create from them—to activate a kind of flywheel of continually reflecting, noticing, and knowing our feelings in order to honor the contexts that offered space for them to emerge. We need not keep this essential and profound understanding to ourselves. Remember to feel it and to share it. And keep going.

Resources

A book is a snapshot of a moment in time. Please visit designforbelonging.com and follow #DesignForBelonging to see further thinking and toolkits on this topic. The following list of books, tools, and organizations is an expanded set of host-heroes offering support for your journey.

Books for Exploring Belonging

Agrawal, Radha. *Belong: Find Your People, Create Community, and Live a More Connected Life.* New York: Workman Publishing, 2018.

Benjamin, Ruha. *Race After Technology: Abolitionist Tools for the New Jim Code.* Medford, MA: Polity Press, 2019.

Benson, Tracey, and Sarah Fiarman. *Unconscious Bias in Schools: A Developmental Approach to Exploring Race and Racism.* Cambridge, MA: Harvard Education Press, 2020.

Birdsong, Mia. *How We Show Up: Reclaiming Family, Friendship, and Community.* New York: Hachette Books, 2020.

brown, adrienne maree. *Pleasure Activism: The Politics of Feeling Good.* Chico, CA: AK Press, 2019.

brown, adrienne maree. *Emergent Strategy: Shaping Change, Changing Worlds.* Chico, CA: AK Press, 2017.

Buettner, Dan. *The Blue Zones of Happiness: Lessons from the World's Happiest People.* Washington, DC: National Geographic, 2017.

Carroll, Kevin. *A Kids Book About Belonging*. Portland, OR: A Kids Book About, 2019.

Hammond, Zaretta. *Culturally Responsive Teaching and the Brain: Promoting Authentic Engagement and Rigor Among Culturally and Linguistically Diverse Students*. Thousand Oaks, CA: Corwin, 2015.

Kaur, Valerie. *See No Stranger: A Memoir and Manifesto of Revolutionary Love*. New York: Penguin Random House, 2020.

Menakem, Resmaa. *My Grandmother's Hands: Racialized Trauma and the Pathway to Mending Our Hearts and Bodies*. Las Vegas, NV: Central Recovery Press, 2017.

Murthy, Vivek H. *Together: The Healing Power of Human Connection in a Sometimes Lonely World*. New York: HarperCollins, 2020.

Parker, Priya. *The Art of Gathering: How We Meet and Why It Matters*. New York: Riverhead Books: 2018.

Selassie, Sebene. *You Belong: A Call for Connection*. New York: HarperCollins, 2020.

Spinks, David. *The Business of Belonging: How to Make Community Your Competitive Advantage*. Hoboken, NJ: Wiley, 2021.

Turner, Edith. *Communitas: The Anthropology of Collective Joy*. New York: Palgrave Macmillan, 2012.

Turner, Toko-pa. *Belonging: Remembering Ourselves Home*. British Columbia, Canada: Her Own Room Press, 2017.

Vellos, Kat. *We Should Get Together: The Secret to Cultivating Better Friendships*. San Francisco: Katherine Vellos, 2019.

Wheatley, Margaret, and Deborah Frieze. *Walk Out Walk On: A Learning Journey into Communities Daring to Live the Future Now*. San Francisco: Berrett-Koehler Publishers, 2011.

Resources

Books for Exploring Belonging, continued

williams, angel Kyodo, and Rod Owens, with Jasmine Syedullah. *Radical Dharma: Talking Race, Love, and Liberation.* Berkeley, CA: North Atlantic Books, 2016.

Books for Exploring Design

Amabile, Teresa, and Steven Kramer. *The Progress Principle: Using Small Wins to Ignite Joy, Engagement, and Creativity at Work.* Boston: Harvard Business Review Press, 2011.

Constanza-Chock, Sasha. *Design Justice: Community-Led Practices to Build the Worlds We Need.* Cambridge, MA: The MIT Press, 2020.

Cross, Nigel. *Designerly Ways of Knowing.* London: Springer, 2006.

Doorley, Scott, and Scott Witthoft. *Make Space: How to Set the Stage for Creative Collaboration.* Hoboken, NJ: Wiley, 2012.

Escobar, Arturo. *Designs for the Pluriverse: Radical Interdependence, Autonomy, and the Making of Worlds.* Durham, NC: Duke University Press, 2018.

Kleon, Austin. *Steal Like an Artist.* New York: Workman Publishing, 2012.

Lupton, Ellen, and Andrea Lipps. *The Senses: Design Beyond Vision.* New York: Princeton Architectural Press, 2018.

Madson, Patricia Ryan. *Improv Wisdom: Don't Prepare, Just Show Up.* New York: Bell Tower, 2005.

McCloud, Scott. *Understanding Comics.* New York: HarperCollins, 1993.

Ozenc, Kursat, and Margaret Hagan. *Rituals for Work: 50 Ways to Create Engagement, Shared Purpose, and a Culture that Can Adapt to Change.* Hoboken, NJ: Wiley, 2019.

Tools to Get Your Hands On

These are interactive card decks to help your design-for-belonging practice move forward.

Anaissie, Tania, Victor Cary, David Clifford, Tom Malarkey, and Susie Wise. *Liberatory Design.* Available at liberatorydesign.com.

Noel, Lesley-Ann. *The Designer's Critical Alphabet.* Available at etsy.com.

Organizations to Explore

Abundant Community
abundantcommunity.com

Beytna Design
beytnadesign.com

Center for Anti-Racist Education
antiracistfuture.org

Chi by Design
chibydesign.com

Creative Reaction Lab
creativereactionlab.com

Design School X
designschoolx.org

Equity Meets Design
equitymeetsdesign.com

Greater Good Science Center
greatergood.berkeley.edu

Inclusion Design Group
inclusiondesign.com

National Equity Project
nationalequityproject.org

Othering & Belonging Institute
belonging.berkeley.edu

Playworks
playworks.org

Reflex Design Collective
reflexdesigncollective.com

Restore Commons
restorecommons.com

Student Experience
Research Network
studentexperiencenetwork.org

Studio Pathways
studiopathways.org

Weave: The Social Fabric Project
weareweavers.org/about

Bibliography

Anaissie, T., Cary, V., Clifford, D., Malarkey, T., and Wise, S. *Liberatory Design*. http://www.liberatorydesign.com, 2021.

Block, Peter. *Community: The Structure of Belonging.* San Francisco: Berrett-Koehler, 2008.

Brown, Brené. *Braving the Wilderness: The Quest for True Belonging and the Courage to Stand Alone.* New York: Penguin Random House, 2017.

Brown, Brené. *Unlocking Us*, "Podcast interview with Laverne Cox," June 17, 2020. https://brenebrown.com/podcast/brene-with-laverne -cox-on-transgender-representation-advocacy-the-power-of-love/

Ewing, Eve L. "I'm a Black Scholar Who Studies Race. Here's Why I Capitalize 'White.'" July 1, 2020. https://zora.medium.com /im-a-black-scholar-who-studies-race-here-s-why-i-capitalize -white-f94883aa2dd3

Farrington, Camille. *Failing at School: Lessons for Redesigning Urban High Schools.* New York: Teachers College Press, 2014.

Finney, Carolyn. *Black Faces, White Spaces: Reimagining the Relationship of African Americans to the Great Outdoors.* Chapel Hill: The University of North Carolina Press, 2014.

Goodman, Amy. "How His Hit Movie 'Sorry to Bother You' Slams Capitalism & Offers Solutions." Interview with Boots Riley. *Democracy Now*, July 17, 2018. https://www.democracynow .org/2018/7/17/boots_riley_on_how_his_hit

Hannah-Jones, Nikole. "It Is Time for Reparations." *New York Times Magazine*, June 24, 2020.

Healey, Kaleen, and Stroman, Chloe. "Structures for Belonging: A Synthesis of Research on Belonging-Supportive Learning Environments," February 2021. studentexperienceproject.org.

Holmes, Kat. *Mismatch: How Inclusion Shapes Design.* Cambridge, MA: The MIT Press, 2018.

hooks, bell. *Belonging: A Culture of Place.* New York: Routledge, 2009.

powell, john a., and Mendian, Stephen. "The Problem of Othering: Towards Inclusiveness and Belonging." In *Othering and Belonging: Expanding the Circle of Human Concern,* Issue One, Summer 2016. https://otheringandbelonging.org/issue-1/

Romero, Carissa. "What We Know About Belonging from Scientific Research," July 2015. studentexperienceproject.org.

Steele, Claude M. *Whistling Vivaldi: How Stereotypes Affect Us and What We Can Do.* New York: Norton, 2010.

Tough, Paul. "Who Gets to Graduate?" *New York Times Magazine,* May 2014.

Tough, Paul. *The Years That Matter Most: How College Makes or Breaks Us.* New York: Houghton Mifflin Harcourt, 2019.

Wheatley, Margaret. *Leadership and the New Science: Discovering Order in a Chaotic World,* 3rd ed. San Francisco: Berrett-Koehler, 2006.

Yap, Christine Wong. *100 Stories of Belonging in the S.F. Bay Area.* Berkeley: Haas Institute for a Fair and Inclusive Society at UC Berkeley, 2019.

Yeager, David S., and Walton, Gregory M. "Teaching a Lay Theory Before College Narrows Achievement Gaps at Scale." *Proceedings of the National Academy of Sciences* 113(24), May 2016.

Yeager, David S., Walton, Gregory M., and Cohen, Geoffrey L. "Addressing Achievement Gaps with Psychological Interventions." *Phi Delta Kappan* 94(5), February 2013.

Acknowledgments

My only way to write a book—even a "little book," as this project is called—was to do work in the world. Some seeds were planted before the book got underway. Thanks to Jamie Allison; you and your Cowell Foundation team were the first to invite me to work on the intersection of design and belonging. Thanks to the K12 Lab team and, especially, Ariel Raz, David Clifford, and Devon Young for jumping in to build with me and to Durell Coleman and Tania Anaissie for joining us to make it happen. Mara Benitez, your work with me on School Retool equity design frameworks was foundational as well. Thank you for your thought partnership. Mariah Rankine-Landers, you told me about the Othering + Belonging conference back in 2017. It had just occurred, so I kept a sticky note up until it came around again in 2019. You and your Studio Pathways work are an inspiration; thank you.

I am so grateful for the many people who supported me to host workshops and try out tools and activities once the book project was underway. I'm naming the people who invited me; please know that my gratitude extends to their entire teams. Thanks to Kate Canales and the team for my "micro-residency" at the UT Design Department. Thanks also to CCB, Kate Rancourt, and Trevor Croghan at One WorkPlace, Laura Cole at the

Monarch Experience, Lauren Hancock and Amanda Otte at the SJ Learns Community of Practice, Liz Gerber and DeYandré Thaxton at the Segal Institute of Design, Heather Dermott at Idaho Business for the Outdoors, Adam Weiler at Steelcase Social Innovation, Jill Vialet and our Workswell effort, Morgan Vien for prototyping at the Carnegie Summit twice (and may your stoke continue to spread!), and Jen Goldstein and the students of Design for Belonging: Autism Care; you slid in at the end of this process but played an important role. Always in the mix was the influence of the Liberatory Design Crew. To David Clifford, Tania Anaissie, Tom Malarkey, and Victor Cary, please know that I am forever indebted and honored by your willingness to collaborate with me. Early versions of tools I crafted with Abby VanMuijen, Lala Openi, and Tom Maiorana; I am grateful to each of you for your willingness to play.

Heather Tsavaris, the first time we met, we talked about belonging. Your vision has given me fuel when I had little. Sadly, BOB didn't quite make it (yet), but your partnership and collaborative spirit have been incredible. To all our sprint partners, co-designers, and the DSS team, your work continues to motivate me.

Critical to all these contributing projects and prototypes was spending 2019 through 2020 as an inaugural fellow with the Mira Fellowship. I am grateful to my coaches Co Barry, Kai Barry, and Sara Heintzelman, as well as my fellow fellows Betty Ray, Eleanor Kane, Marc Mares, and Travis Ning; your willingness to ask me what I meant was invaluable. And to the 2021 fellows, Jalyn Gordon, Lin Shi, Morgan Vien, Naomi Stone, and Nita Evans, welcome to the family!

In addition to exploring the book through work in the world, I learned about writing as a daily practice. I learned this first from my dissertation advisor Sam Wineburg and know I would not have had the confidence to try this project if I had not been taught by him. This work was sustained in real time by a writing group that I met with most days on Zoom. It was started by Christine Ortiz and then maintained by Ela Ben-Ur, Jill Vialet, Julia Kramer, and Tracey Benson. Here's to writing in fifty-minute chunks and positive self-talk. The whole idea for this d.school series was generated from a very fun season of exploration. Thanks to Andrea Small, Ashish Goel, Carissa Carter, Molly Wilson, and Scott Witthoft for being part of that endeavor. I am immensely grateful that our steadfast d.school leader Sarah Stein Greenberg was all in as well. The series vision was spearheaded by the one and only Scott Doorley and the ever-sparkling Charlotte Burgess-Auburn. Such deep, deep gratitude to both of you. And way to go; you made a whole lot of books! Not only did you kick this off, but you also had the wisdom to bring in Jenn Brown as an editor. Jenn, your careful attention made me believe I could keep going. You joined us at just the right moment, and I thank you for your infinite calm.

This book would not be what it is without the incredible illustrations of Rose Jaffe. Thank you from the bottom of my heart for bringing your beautiful way of honoring people and their belonging to this endeavor. At Ten Speed Press, Julie Bennett and Emma Campion: what a pleasure to learn about this craft from you.

In addition to all these writing supports, I have several crews I need to thank. Hattie and Frazer, you are the rock where I moor today and every day. Thank you is just one way to say how much you mean to me. To my family, Mom and Mike, Dad, Bec, John and Jennifer, and Dan: thank you for making me who I am. To my Friday #covidtimes happy hour crew: y'all are the best. Thank you for belonging along with me during these unprecedented times. Here's looking at you: Amy Hillyard, Corey Weinstein, Deb Gauck, Hanna Kerns, Jenny Lou Lytton, Kate Baldus, Katie Kramer, Katie Krummeck, Katherine Emery, Kathy Glass, Laura Mann, Liz Gerber, Sheila O'Rourke, and Tana Johnson. Thanks to Dee MacDonald for sharing your space when I needed it and to Peter Worth and Victoria Olsen for early reads. I must also thank longtime mentors and friends Kristina Hooper-Woolsey, Peter Samis, and Sandy Speicher. Finally, for planting the seed that books are a thing one could do, all my love to Christina Boufis, Laura Mann, Lisa Nakamura, Tina Olsen, and Vicky Olsen for the nearly thirty-years-strong Reading Group (aka the RG!).

Index

Library of Congress Cataloging-in-Publication Data
Names: Wise, Susie, author.
Title: Design for belonging : how to build inclusion and collaboration
    in your communities / Susie Wise, Stanford d. School ; illustrations
    by Rose Jaffe.
Description: First Edition. | Emeryville, California : Ten Speed Press, 2022. |
    Includes bibliographical references and index.
Identifiers: LCCN 2021017019 (print) | LCCN 2021017020 (ebook) |
    ISBN 9781984858030 (trade paperback) |
    ISBN 9781984858023 (ebook)
Subjects: LCSH: Social integration. | Marginality, Social. | Communities.
Classification: LCC HM683 .W57 2022 (print) | LCC HM683 (ebook) |
    DDC 305.5/68—dc23
LC record available at https://lccn.loc.gov/2021017019
LC ebook record available at https://lccn.loc.gov/2021017020

Trade Paperback ISBN: 978-1-9848-5803-0
eBook ISBN: 978-1-9848-5802-3

Printed in China

Acquiring editor: Hannah Rahill | Editor: Julie Bennett
Art director and designer: Emma Campion | Production designers: Mari Gill
    and Faith Hague
Typefaces: Hope Meng's d.sign, Grilli Type's GT Super Display, and Dinamo's Whyte
Production manager: Jane Chinn
Copyeditor: Kristi Hein | Proofreader: Lisa Brousseau | Indexer: Michael Goldstein
Publicist: David Hawk | Marketers: Daniel Wikey and Windy Dorresteyn
d.school creative team: Charlotte Burgess-Auburn,
    Scott Doorley, and Nariman (Nadia) Gathers

10 9 8 7 6 5

First Edition